Indigenous
Theology
and the
Western
Worldview

Acadia Studies in Bible and Theology

H. Daniel Zacharias, General Editor

The last several decades have witnessed dramatic developments in biblical and theological study. Full-time academics can scarcely keep up with fresh discoveries, ongoing archaeological work, new exegetical proposals, experiments in methods and hermeneutics, the rise of majority world theology, and innovative theological proposals and syntheses. For students and nonspecialists, these developments can be confusing and daunting. What has been needed is a series of succinct studies that assess these issues and present their findings in a way that students, pastors, laity, and nonspecialists will find accessible and rewarding. Acadia Studies in Bible and Theology, sponsored by Acadia Divinity College in Wolfville, Nova Scotia, and in conjunction with the college's Hayward Lectureship, constitutes such a series.

The Hayward Lectureship has brought to Acadia many distinguished scholars of Bible and theology, such as Sir Robin Barbour, James D. G. Dunn, C. Stephen Evans, Edith Humphrey, Leander Keck, Helmut Koester, Richard Longenecker, Martin Marty, Jaroslav Pelikan, John Webster, Randy Woodley, and N. T. Wright. Initiated by Lee M. McDonald and Craig A. Evans, the Acadia Studies in Bible and Theology series continues to reflect this rich heritage and foundation.

These studies are designed to guide readers through the ever more complicated maze of critical, interpretative, and theological discussion taking place today. But these studies are not introductory in nature; nor are they mere surveys. Authored by leading authorities in the field, books in the Acadia Studies in Bible and Theology series offer critical assessments of major issues that the church faces in the twenty-first century. Readers will gain the requisite orientation and fresh understanding of the important issues that will enable them to take part meaningfully in discussion and debate.

Indigenous Theology
and the
Western Worldview

A Decolonized Approach to Christian Doctrine

Randy S. Woodley

Baker Academic
a division of Baker Publishing Group
Grand Rapids, Michigan

Published by Baker Academic
a division of Baker Publishing Group
PO Box 6287, Grand Rapids, MI 49516-6287
www.bakeracademic.com

Printed in the United States of America

Library of Congress Cataloging-in-Publication Data
Names: Woodley, Randy, 1956– author.
Title: Indigenous theology and the western worldview : a decolonized approach to Christian doctrine / Randy S. Woodley.
Description: Grand Rapids, Michigan : Baker Academic, a division of Baker Publishing Group, [2022] | Series: Acadia studies in Bible and theology | Includes index
Identifiers: LCCN 2021033773 | ISBN 9781540964717 (paperback) | ISBN 9781540964724 (casebound) | ISBN 9781493433414 (ebook) | ISBN 9781493433421 (pdf)
Subjects: LCSH: Postcolonial theology. | Theology. | Indians of North America—Religion.
Classification: LCC BT83.593 .W66 2022 | DDC 230—dc23
LC record available at https://lccn.loc.gov/2021033773ISBN: 9781540964717

Baker Publishing Group publications use paper produced from sustainable forestry practices and post-consumer waste whenever possible.

24   25   26   27   28   7   6   5   4   3

To the Indigenous elders
who took the time to help me find my way:
Joe, Libby and Jake, Madison and Geraldine, Isabell, Gaitha,
Lawrence, Mose, Elmer, Reeves and Clydia, Robert, Dave
and Judy, Stanley and Elaina, Joanne and Teresa, Vincent,
Jerry, Cornel, and many others along the way

Contents

Preface   ix

Acknowledgments   xiii

Opening Interview   1

1. The Myths of History and Progressive Civilizations   9
   Question and Response   44

2. Comparing Western and Indigenous Worldviews   53
   Question and Response   75

3. Decolonizing Western Christian Theology   89
   Question and Response   107

Closing Interview   119

Index   135

Preface

Pedagogy

As a way of setting a proper context for the book, it is necessary that I mention a few particularities concerning an Indigenous pedagogy, which is rooted in Indigenous values. Even the word *pedagogy* implies teaching from a place of unequal positions or the problem of the subject/object paradigm. You will notice the dialogical nature of my style, especially in the question and response sections following each chapter. I feel that, when teaching or presenting, it is paramount to hear all the other voices in the room, not just my own. Although the Hayward Lectures are created in a very Western style, I tried to bend that style toward a more Indigenous platform. The word *pedagogy* technically implies a learning style resembling an adult teaching a child. Pedagogy implies that one person, the teacher or adult, has knowledge to share with the other, the receiver or child. In my graduate and undergraduate courses, I have always referenced my students (another word that implies the former inequality of position) as co-learners. Co-learners, short for "collaborative learners," implies we are positionally equal, learning together. Yes, I likely have more years of study in the subject matter than many of them, but knowledge, not applied, does us little good. I have found that most learning experiences stick best when we bring not just knowledge but our own truth and experience to the conversation. As co-learners apply the knowledge that I help them bring forth, making it real in their own contexts, we learn from one another. Thus, real knowledge, that which is real to each one's experience, is shared together as co-learners in collaboration with the subject matter.

Much has been written about adult learning or what some of us call "anthrogogy," and I need not repeat it here.[1] Master teachers such as Paulo Freire, bell hooks, and Myles Horton have influenced my teaching style, but suffice it to say, the ideas of democracy and teaching from an egalitarian anthrogogy were on this continent long before Europeans arrived. Indigenous teaching styles embody a respect for co-learning without diminishing the authority of the teacher and without objectification of the co-learners. I always cherish conversations when people speak from their hearts, even if I disagree with them. Over the years, I have learned to face a reality in my own life—namely, there are few areas in which I have no opinions or at least have no leanings, and therefore my assumptions are best challenged in groups by others who are thinking on the topic in a different way.

In many of our Native American traditions we have a prayer that often goes something like, "Have pity/understanding on me Creator and remember, I am just a human being." The idea behind this prayer is that perfection is the enemy of attainment.

---

1. Just a few of those who compare adult learners with children include Marie Battiste, *Reclaiming Indigenous Voice and Vision* (Vancouver: University of British Columbia Press, 2000); Donald L. Fixico, *The American Indian Mind in a Linear World* (New York: Routledge, 2013).

We are all simply human beings, imperfect but learning from our mistakes. Those mistakes make us human. And being human by climbing out on a limb in order to reach others is the most spiritual state of being in which we may find ourselves. When those special moments come, everyone in the room feels like we have experienced something together that is truly sacred. Perhaps promoting knowledge among co-learners in an atmosphere of sacred space is the most important role I have as a scholar and a spiritual leader.

Narrative

In this book you will also notice what may seem to some to be an abundance of stories, both of a traditional Indigenous style and my own personal stories. Narrative theology, like anthrogogy, has been used as a primary communication tool among Indigenous peoples from time immemorial. Traditions are passed on orally, often through story, reinforcing the values developed over time among Indigenous peoples. Included in those values is an understanding that spoken words have primordial power. Tribal stories, then, are considered sacred and are not to be used lightly. These sacred stories reinforce other Indigenous values, much in the way ceremony and songs do. Naturally, stories, both shared tribal stories and one's own personal stories, are a primary vehicle for teaching and sustaining life.

In juxtaposition, most Western communicative practices rely on story as a filler or as a way of emphasizing propositional communications. The idea is that brief propositions, especially those alliterated, are an efficient communication tool. Unfortunately, humans do not seem to find themselves in propositions well. Yet they do find themselves in story. As a former pastor, I can objectively say that the message was rarely taken to heart through my days of propositional communication but people always found themselves in story in a personal and practical way. Often forgetting the sermon, they would remark on the earlier children's story. Story has been a primary communication tool among Indigenous people all over the world for that reason, and it is for that reason that I use stories here.

Biography

I chose to begin with the biographical section of the Hayward Lectures called "The Red Couch Conversation" (although I found the couch to be more of a burnt orange color). Traditionally among Indigenous North Americans, when introducing ourselves we are supposed to tell who our people are and where we are from. Tribes such as the Navajo have even formalized this process. Not only does this practice give the listener an idea of who the person is and who the people are from whence they come, but it grounds them in a particular place. Granted, in a very transitory society of mass and frequent migrations, this practice proves itself to be difficult.

Part of the colonial project is to universalize place and uproot our particularities and blur our homage to a particular place. In an integration of both place-based and relational theologies, I try to tell the story of my own identity and sense of place. Hopefully, it will matter to you how who I am relates to what and how I teach. We are all, in many ways, influenced by our environment. We owe it to those people and those places to recall their important effect on our lives.

Acknowledgments

I'd like to acknowledge the support of my cohort and other Indigenous friends whose lives and questions caused me to think better and to become a better human being: Edith Engavo Woodley (Eastern Shoshone), Adrian Jacobs (Cayuga), Richard Twiss (Lakota), Ray Aldred (Plains Cree), Fern Cloud (Dakota), Terry LeBlanc (Miqmaq), Glenn Pedro (Arapaho/Cheyenne), Lenore Three Stars (Lakota), John White Eagle (Southern Cheyenne), Wa-do equah! I'd also like to acknowledge a few people whom I did not know but who struggled with the same type of questions early on, including Black Elk (Lakota), Ohiyesa/Charles Eastman (Dakota), and Jesse Bushyhead (Cherokee).

Opening Interview

The following conversation took place as part of the Red Couch Conversation in conjunction with the MacRae Centre for Faith and Culture.

How would you introduce yourself if someone asked, "Who is Randy Woodley?"

Well, in our Keetoowah tradition, I was taught we're not actually supposed to talk about ourselves, so I wouldn't introduce myself if I had the choice, but I can do so here. I would say, first of all, that my wife and I are farmer/planters, and we grow our food and seeds, so that others can grow their own food.

And, if someone asked, "Why are you giving lectures? Are you lecturing on food?"

I would say, I can't understand why people keep asking me to give lectures!

What is your role at Portland Seminary?

I received tenure a couple years ago, and then this year I moved down to three-quarter time, and for the next several years I'm teaching online only. I wanted to begin to transition from a more academic setting to a more accessible setting for our

Indigenous people and for others who want to think differently. You know, academia is good in some ways. It is supposed to open us to new ideas and all that, but our original vision at Eloheh Indigenous Center for Earth Justice[1] was to reach people who really can't afford a formal education or who aren't able to enroll because of adverse life conditions or other reasons that prevent them from undertaking the rigors of academia. So, that's the type of education we want to get back to. I guess I have climbed the academic mountain, stood at the top, and looked over the whole enterprise, and now I'm coming back down on the other side.

Can you tell us where you grew up and how you came to meet Jesus?

I'm from the United States. They say my third great-grandfather was a Chickamaugan chief who fought against the United States in a nineteen-year war and then made peace with them. In my own background I have mixed loyalties, I guess you'd say. I'm also a person on two sides of the American culture. Both my parents are assimilated mixed-blood Cherokees, so I'm a person who has all through his life struggled with identity. I think a lot of Native folks, and also just people in general, struggle with identity. We're always in this fast-moving, cosmopolitan, urbanized world, coming to understand differently who we are at different times. Most of us don't have the luxury of remaining in one place anymore, and so it's been a unique process for me to understand who I am. So, when you start asking those identity questions, the answers could get long and involved. But I guess I'll start with my parents.

---

1. "Indigenous Center for Earth Justice," Eloheh, accessed May 24, 2021, www
.eloheh.org.

My Dad is a veteran of World War II. After the tragedy of Pearl Harbor, he left his parents' farm in Mississippi the day after he graduated high school, and he joined the Navy. When the war was over, he moved to Birmingham, Alabama, to his sister's home, got a delivery job at Sears, and met my mom. Mom was working at the Sears candy counter. My mom's people were very poor. She was raised in the coal mining camps. She had to quit school when she was thirteen and move to the city to live with an aunt, so she could work and send money back home to her family. She was the oldest daughter. Her older brothers didn't have to do that, just the girls—totally unfair.

Just a little digression here. I was speaking a few weeks ago to a congregation I'd never met before, and I said, "You know, women are smarter than men, right?" They looked at me quizzically, and I said, "You know how I know that?" And one of our female friends who was there yelled out, "Because Edith told you!" Okay, I agreed, but the thing about women being smarter in life, of course, is what anthropologists call Indigenous Cosmopolitanism. This refers to the ability to understand and act from two different worldviews or the ability to operate in multiple ethnic cultures. But, I thought to myself, unfortunately, it's still a "man's world" and women are oppressed, still being denied equal rights or fair treatment. Women have had to think with both a male and a female worldview all along in order to make it in this world. Men, well, we have the privilege of just having to think like men. As a result, women must be smarter than men.

I am an Indigenous Cosmopolitan; one who can operate in both a Western worldview and an Indigenous worldview. I was exposed to both cultures, and other cultures as well, throughout most of my life. My folks got married, and they became part of what historians call the Great Migration, which was, as it's thought of sociologically, the movement of six million Black people from the rural South pouring to cities in the North, Midwest, and West for work in factories and other somewhat demeaning jobs, but with much better pay than they had previously. But it wasn't just Black people in the migration. There were a lot of poor Native Americans, Whites, and others who also migrated. My dad went to work for Ford Motor Company, and after a while he saved enough money to start his own seat-cover business, working for himself while still in the booming automobile industry. He made seat covers for seventeen years, and then he became a home builder, still owning his own business. Early on, my mother went to beauty school and became a beautician.

I first went to school in a place called Willow Run, Michigan, which is outside of Ypsilanti, which is outside of Ann Arbor. Most people know where Ann Arbor is because it's home to the University of Michigan, but Ypsilanti is sort of the underside of Ann Arbor, and then Willow Run is the underside of Ypsilanti. I grew up in a very rough and poor place. Willow Run was multiracial, multicultural, and multiethnic, with lots of working-class poor. I was able to garner a wider perspective than many of the people I met later in life as a result of this social and cultural richness. All this diversity led me to have a passion for understanding other people, especially people different from me. I was a typical teenager of the '60s and '70s in that I was highly involved in drugs and rock 'n' roll bands and all those things. I met Jesus at age ten, and then again when I was nineteen. I went to Eastern Michigan University in Ypsilanti on the pass/fail program, but I flunked out my first semester. So I'm a PhD who is also a flunky. Maybe some people will be encouraged by that.

I wanted to move back home when I flunked out, and I asked my parents if I could, and they said, "Maybe!" Now, my folks are Baptist and Baptists are big among Cherokee. I have a friend who is a traditional Cherokee stomp dancer, and he half-jokingly says that the Baptists have been around us for so long that Cherokees just consider them one of our traditional religions.

My parents' church had just had a revival. In the United States, Baptists bring a preacher in once a year in the fall for a week of preaching revival meetings. It was October, and I had just missed their revival meetings. My folks were probably thinking the whole time, "If we could have just got Randy here, he could have been saved!" So they saw their opportunity when I was flunking out of school and asked to move back home. They told me I could move back home on one condition: I must promise to go to the revival with them the next fall. Okay, I said. Simple enough, right?

I didn't know it then, but my mom was organizing people praying for me all over the world! And for me, that year was the roughest year of my life! I had a drug overdose, some of my friends were killed, and a family member was killed, and after one long, hellish year, it was finally the last night of the revival, and I promised them I'd go, and they wouldn't take no for an answer. So I finally got in the car with them, and this is how I know the Spirit is real, because about the time I shut the car door, my heart started pounding in my throat. And by the time I got to the church, it was pounding so loud I thought other people might even be able to hear it. And by the time the altar call came, well, I don't even remember walking down to the altar. I think I might have actually floated down the aisle!

I had known Jesus as a younger child, having been intro-duced at ten years old at a church camp. I was led to Christ then by a full-blooded Ojibwa man. I was probably just as fascinated with him as I was with Jesus at the time because we were all mixed-bloods, and I wanted to see what "real Indians" were like! I spent a lot of time with him that week of camp and in the end, he led me to Jesus. He also taught me to harvest sassafras and steer a canoe.

So, at nineteen, I'm actually coming back to Jesus, and I just want to be left alone to pray. I spent maybe forty-five minutes to an hour back there in a back room praying, and the only thing I remember is that I said, "Jesus, if you can deliver me from these drugs"—because I hadn't been able to get off them by myself—"I'll follow you the rest of my life, and I'll never look back." And it felt like I got hit on the head with a sledgehammer. Then I got up, and I walked away, and I knew that Jesus was real, and I knew that my life was going to be different from that point on. And it was! I went to all my friends, and I told them I couldn't hang with them anymore, that I was following Jesus and needed to change. Some of them said, "Well, good for you." Following Jesus took me on a series of journeys all around the country, doing stuff like marrying a very interesting person named Edith. Now we've got four kids and five grandkids.

My parents were farmers or planters of a sort. When you come from farmers or gardeners who had gardens the size of some people's farms, farming and gardening just come naturally. I grew up with that, and so there was always the love of the earth and the love for watching things grow. When Edith and I got married, well, we discovered that farming and gardening weren't very natural for her. Edith was raised on the Wind River Indian Reservation in Wyoming, and her family had horses and cattle, but I had this vegetable background, and so we eventually merged those two backgrounds together and became farmers. We now have our own seed company, and we are trying to preserve open-pollinated, organic seeds, many native species, and heirloom seeds, and that's all very important to us. I would say every bit as important as our theological work because I don't see a difference between them. I guess that's me.

How do you go from the background you described to becoming a theologian? Do you identify as a theologian, and at what point did you decide to or decide not to?

I like to say that everyone is a theologian. It's just that some are good, and some are not so good.

What determines good and not so good?

Perhaps how well we understand who God is? My academic training is really in missiology, and I've always had a love of church history. I've always loved thinking about these things. I try to think deeply about everything, and so if you're a follower of Jesus, that also helps us. I fell in love with a lot of the stories in scripture and just wanted to understand those more. Because I think deeply about God, some people call me a theologian. I think the way that my theology may be different from other people's is that, for me, everything begins with the earth and then we go from there.

1

The Myths of History and Progressive Civilizations

Seeking a Blessing on Indigenous Land

One of the things that was said in the introduction to the Hayward Lectures that made me feel quite at home were the words *disruptive ideas*.[1] The Hayward Lectures seek to amplify "disruptive ideas." When I heard that I thought, "Oh, good! I can be myself in these lectures." Thanks to Danny Zacharias and the rest of the folks, the Hayward family and others who've invited me here and especially to Tammy, the local Indigenous representative who welcomed us to this land. It's an honor to be in this beautiful land.

Edith and I travel a lot and have done so for years. We spent four years where we just traveled around from reservation to

---

1. "The Hayward Lectures advances its vision by inviting world-class scholars to Acadia in the aforementioned disciplines to address the community each October on their freshest work and emerging or disruptive ideas in the formats of lecture, conversation, and writing." "Hayward Lectures," Acadia Divinity College, accessed June 15, 2021, www.acadiadiv.ca/hayward-lectures/.

reservation across the United States and Canada and mentored a number of people. We also did a lot of speaking during those four years. We homeschooled our kids, and we had the rich experience of our whole family being around all kinds of Native people from almost everywhere on Turtle Island.[2] Those were probably the richest experiences of our lives.

We've been doing Native American work, serving our own Indigenous peoples, for over thirty years. I consider those years the most valuable times among all my learning experiences. I'm going to share a story with you from those years because I know Canada has a wonderful practice of recognizing the host peoples of the land. Wherever we went to speak, we always sought the blessing of the host people whose land we were on because that's what we were taught by our elders. So we were going to the Ojibwa reservation near Hayward, Wisconsin. When I got there, I asked the group that had invited me, the YWAM Native leadership base, "Who welcomed you on the land?"

They had invited us to come up for a week and teach an Indigenous Leadership course, so I wanted to be sure all was being done in a good way. Unfortunately, no one had really invited them on the land, so I said, "Well then, we can't speak." This type of problem has actually happened a couple of different times, but we've always been able to work through it. Creator has always made a way for us to receive the local blessing and speak. But in Hayward, we had just learned of the problem, so we had to tell our host that we won't speak unless the host people welcome us somehow.

Now, it just so happened that day that this young Ojibwa kid from Seattle, not yet in his twenties, was hitchhiking on the

2. *The Canadian Encyclopedia*, s.v. "Turtle Island," by Amanda Robinson, last modified November 6, 2018, www.thecanadianencyclopedia.ca/en/article/turtle-island.

reservation. The young man and his brother were adopted out when he was about two years old and were raised in Seattle by a White family. He had recently experienced an LSD trip where he saw Jesus, and Jesus told him, "I want you to go back to your reservation." The young man knew he was from a reservation somewhere, way out in Wisconsin. Well, it just so happened that the director of the YWAM base saw him hitchhiking on the road and picked him up. The director asked him if he knew who his people were, but he did not. He told Dave, the director of the YWAM base, that while on LSD, Jesus told him to come out here. Then Dave asked if he had any place to stay. He did not. Dave told him he could stay with them, so they fed him and gave him shelter. We got there later that same day.

Naturally, I took the opportunity to include this Ojibwe young man and had him stick with me all that day so he could learn something from it. I knew enough to know that he wasn't there by accident. "I want to teach you some things," I told him, and he said, "Okay." I told him whenever we go to someone else's land, even now, my elders told me, even when driving down the road, to stop and put tobacco down, because that is someone else's land and we need to respect it. But to be completely honest, I need to tell you that when driving I haven't always done that, just because we travel through so many places, we'd be stopping constantly. But we have asked for permission wherever we teach or exercise any sort of spiritual influence. And so it was important that we do this right that day, especially now that we had a young person trying to find himself and his Indigenous identity. After some thought was given to this, we figured out who the elder was we should speak with. He was one of the two leaders of the Midewiwin Lodge, their tribal religion, and he was also a tribal elder and elder representative to the tribal council.

We went to the local store, and we made a traditional elder basket that consisted of flour and tobacco, a flashlight and coat hangers, sugar and coffee, fresh fruit, and all the kinds of things that elders like. After tracking down his address, we went to his house and knocked on the door, and his wife answered. I guess people visit him often for advice so she very naturally said, "Oh, come in and set the basket down, he's on the phone right now." Finally, he came back and asked respectfully, "Who are you guys and what do you want?" So I explained to him who we were and that we were going to be teaching on spiritual matters to Indigenous leaders there. He said, "Well, what are you going to be teaching?" I explained how we do things according to our traditional teachings, but we follow Jesus. We were calling it "contextual Native ministry" at the time, but I don't really think of it like that anymore. We just live the life we are supposed to be living. Now we're just Indians being Indians.

Then he started telling us some pretty interesting stories. He said, "You know what you all believe and what we believe is not that different?" Then he told us of a couple of subtle differences concerning hell and the devil. He said, "You know, when I was a younger person, I wanted to find out what you Christians believe, so I enrolled for a semester in this college. It's called Moody Bible College, you ever heard of that?" We were surprised and talked about that for some time. But every now and then he would keep interrupting his own story, which meant he was trying to get a point across, and he said, "You know, my uncle told me to never disrespect Jesus, because Jesus is a great spirit and I talk to him." And he would go on and he'd tell us more and more, and then he would say this thing about his uncle again. He told us about how he had just come back from a big meeting of Gichi Dowan, big medicine people from around the United States and Canada. These Ojibwa spiritual leaders were all trying to decide how they could get along better with the Christians. And he told us some stories about all this.

We sat there for maybe two hours, and at least six or seven times he said this thing about his uncle and respecting Jesus. Then at one point he said, "My uncle trained most of the spiritual leaders around this area. He lived to be over a hundred years old, and my uncle would tell me all these stories about Jesus. So I asked my uncle one time, I said, 'Uncle, how do you know all this about Jesus? Did you go to residential school?' He said, 'Oh no! No! I never did that.' Then I asked him, 'Did the priest teach you?' And he says, 'No, I have never been to church.' Then I said, 'But you tell me all the stuff about Jesus. Have you been reading the Bible?' My uncle said, 'No, just remember what I told you in the past: don't disrespect Jesus 'cause he's a great spirit, and I talk to him.' I said to my uncle, 'Well yeah, you talk to him, but how do you know all these things he's done?' You know my uncle looked at me so quizzically, and then he said, 'Well, when I talk to him, of course he talks back.' And then the elder said, 'I'm going to pray for you now,' and then our time was over."

The message was simple to understand: It's just like when I used to pastor and I would tell the children's sermon before the regular sermon. I would tell them, "If you understood the implications of what I just said in the children's story, you don't have to stay for the adult preaching—you can go on home." If you understood the story I just told about the visit with this elder, you understand my message, because it holds the core of it.

Privilege and Heritage

I'll be talking about White privilege in this chapter. But first I will share a bit about my own privilege, because I have some.

We all do. I'm a male, I'm straight, I'm educated, light-skinned, and of copious body size, so I take up a little space in the room. I'm an able-bodied, middle-class, Native American legal descendant recognized by the United Keetoowah Band of Cherokee Indians in Oklahoma. I was raised in a working-class poor family. I'm the first, maybe of a thousand cousins, to get a PhD. We are first-generation non–coal miners, on my mom's side. We come from working-poor, union-organizing people. I was educated later in life. After many years, I finally got my PhD, and I'm feeling it in my body as well as in my mind. I was raised in a very multicultural, multiracial atmosphere, and I've experienced racial oppression in some pretty severe ways at different times and places.

Winston Churchill said, "I consider that it will be found much better . . . to leave the past to history, especially as I propose to write that history myself."[3] He did write history, and it was kind to him. Why? Because whoever interprets history also influences theology and gets to name the myths that underlie a mythologized society, creating them into their own worldview. So "the winners write history," as is often said. I teach my co-learners (students) in our history classes that there is no such thing as history; there are only histories. So even under the best of circumstances, it is often the case that "might makes right."

The following is a quotation from Indigenous Canadian author and professor Taiaiake Alfred.[4] He writes about Indig-

3. Winston Churchill, speech in the House of Commons, delivered January 23, 1948, quoted in *The Yale Book of Quotations*, ed. Fred R. Shapiro (New Haven: Yale University Press, 2006), 154.
4. Gerald Taiaiake Alfred is an educator, author, and activist. He was born in Montreal in 1964. Alfred is an internationally recognized intellectual and political advisor, and he is currently a professor at the University of Victoria. Alfred grew up in Kahnawake and received a BA in history from Concordia University and an MA and a PhD from Cornell. He served in the US Marine Corps in the 1980s. Alfred currently serves as director of the Indigenous Governance Program. He was awarded a

enous education, but I want to substitute the word *religion* for the word *education* for our current context. He states:

> The machinery of Indigenous [religion] may simply replicate European systems. But even if such [religion] resembles traditional Native American systems on the surface, without strong and healthy leaders committed to traditional values and the preservation of our nationhood, they are going to fail. Our children will judge them to have failed because a [religion] that is not based on traditional principles of respect and harmonious coexistence will inevitably tend to reflect the cold, calculating and coercive ways of the modern state. The whole of the decolonization process will have been for nothing if Indigenous [religion] has no meaningful Indigenous character. Worse, if the new [religion] does not embody a notion of power that is appropriate to Indigenous cultures, the goals of the struggle will have been betrayed. Leaders who promote non-Indigenous goals will embody non-Indigenous values and are simply used by the state to maintain its control.[5]

I have seen this happen numerous times in both educational and church spheres.

There is an image created by the University of Tennessee, a rendering of a Cherokee village as it would have looked in its day. Today, that village now lies beneath the Tennessee River.

Canada Research Chair from 2003 to 2007. In addition, he has received a National Aboriginal Achievement Award in education. Among decolonization theorists, Alfred fits closest to Memmi in that he believes the colonizer is as much caught in a trap as the colonized, and both must be liberated. He sees no point in violent revolution, such as is advocated by Frantz Fanon, because it reduces the colonized to the same level as the colonizer. To Alfred, indigenization is the action of freedom that moves one out of victimization.

5. Gerald Taiaiake Alfred, *Peace, Power, Righteousness: An Indigenous Manifesto* (Don Mills, ON: Oxford University Press, 1999), xiv.

Although the town is completely under water now, from the archaeological evidence they were able to reconstruct an image of how it might have looked. The image I'm thinking of is the former town of Tellico. This was one of the villages where my third great-grandfather resided, my ancestors' home. But it's not here anymore, or at least no longer visible, fulfilling the American mythological angst of the disappearing Indian.[6]

When I lived in the American South, I would visit a natural spring every chance I had. As a Cherokee person, I would take my children to water ceremony there. It's called the Blue Hole. The Blue Hole is my favorite sacred place in the world. I won't be able to have my ashes spread there because that's not allowed, as it's a state park, but my place of rest and peace is that spring right there, and those are two things that are very meaningful to me—rest and peace. At this spring, I can think back clearly about who I am and where I come from. The location of the Blue Hole is also the location of one of the last meetings of Cherokees before the removal so it also has sad memories. Rest and peace and sadness and identity can all come together in our Indigenous reality.

Reverend Dr. Martin Luther King Jr. said, "Our nation was born in genocide. We tried, as a matter of national policy, to wipe out its Indigenous population. Moreover, we elevated that tragic experience into a noble crusade. Indeed, even today we have not permitted ourselves to reject or feel remorse for the shameful episode."[7] Canada has moved more on this front than

6. Depictions in literature such as *The Last of the Mohicans* and in art such as *The End of the Trail* show Native Americans as a people who are disappearing. Andrea Smith, "Heteropatriarchy and the Three Pillars of White Supremacy," in *Color of Violence*, ed. INCITE! (Durham, NC: Duke University Press, 2016), 66–73.

7. Martin Luther King Jr., *Why We Can't Wait* (New York: Harper & Row, 1964), 121–22.

the United States in the apology to Indigenous peoples and the process of Truth and Reconciliation.[8]

John F. Kennedy, one of our great and most beloved presidents, said, "For a subject worked and reworked, and one considered so often in novels, motion pictures and television, American Indians remain probably the least understood and most misunderstood Americans of us all. Collectively, their history is our history and should be part of our shared and remembered heritage. When we forget great contributors to our American history, when we neglect the heroic past of the American Indian, we thereby weaken our own heritage. We need to remember the heritage our forefathers found here and from which they borrowed liberally."[9] These are lessons that we're still trying to learn in the United States.

Terrapin and the Wolves

I want to tell you a story, a Chickamaugan story. The Chickamauga are a particular group of Cherokee to which my ancestors belonged. When the "Revolutionary War" broke out, about half of our Cherokee people remained neutral. The other half fought with the British. Among those who fought with the British, and who continued to fight for seventeen years after the British surrendered, were my ancestors who were Chickamaugans. From what I can surmise, my third and fourth great-grandfathers fought in the Revolutionary War against tyranny—against the United States! So that group became what's known as the Chickamaugans, and those are my people.

8. See Truth and Reconciliation Commission of Canada, *A Knock on the Door: The Essential History of Residential Schools from the Truth and Reconciliation Commission of Canada* (Winnipeg: University of Manitoba Press, 2016).

9. John F. Kennedy, quoted in Alvin M. Josephy, ed., *The American Heritage Book of Indians*, 3rd ed. (New York: American Heritage, 1961), 7.

We have a story among the Chickamauga, and it goes like this.[10] You know what a Terrapin is; sometimes it is called a box turtle. Chickamaugans use the box turtle shells for several of our ceremonies, for shakers and for our dances. A long time ago, the Terrapin was a whole lot bigger than it is now. Terrapin was a great warrior, and he would walk down the road and he would expect everybody to move out of the road for him. One day a Wolf was coming down the same road as Terrapin, but the wolf said to himself, "You know, I've had enough! This time, I'm not getting out of Terrapin's way at all. He's going to have to move me if he wants me to move." So sure enough, Wolf walked by and Terrapin says, "Move out of my way," but the Wolf says, "I'm not moving!" So Terrapin just grabbed ahold of that Wolf and killed him in no time flat.

I heard that's the first reported incident of road rage. So Terrapin takes Wolf and he cut his ears off and he puts them on his belt, and he starts walking. Now Terrapin is getting pretty hungry by this time and the first village he comes to he's thinking, "I'm going to make those people feed me and give me a place to sleep for the night." Well, it happened that the first town he came to was Wolf Town, so Terrapin goes in and tells the wolves what to do for him. He says, "I'm hungry. I want some stew," and they were all afraid of Terrapin because he had such a bad reputation, so they went and got him some stew. Well, then Terrapin pulls out those two wolf ears from his belt, and he begins just shoveling the stew with them, using them like spoons, one after the other. The wolves recognize those ears, and they said, "That's our brother's ears! We have got to do something about this!" But

10. Told as I recall from my friend Robert Francis at an Eloheh time of teaching/learning in Nicholasville, Kentucky, in 2005.

they were all afraid of Terrapin, so they decided to make a careful plan.

Terrapin went to sleep that night, but when he woke up the next day the whole village was gone—it was empty. So Terrapin was walking along out of the village, and suddenly they all jumped out from behind the rocks, and they threw some rope around Terrapin and they said, "We got him now!" And, of course, Terrapin deserved everything he was going to get, but their plan only went so far. "What are we going to do now?" one wolf asked. Another one of the wolves said, "You know what we should do? We should put him in a big clay pot and boil him up and eat him." Terrapin was listening to them, and he said, "If you do that, I'm going to kick that pot to pieces. That's going to put the fire out and then I'm going to come out and I'm going to kill every one of you!" So they thought, "Well, maybe that's not such a good idea."

Another wolf suggested they tie him to a stake and then burn him alive. So Terrapin once again heard them talking and laughed to himself, and he said, "Yeah, you do that and I'll let the fire burn through the ropes. Then I'm going to take these ropes off and I'm going to jump out of that fire and I'm going to kill every one of you!" So the wolves are thinking, "What are we going to do?" And then one of them gets the idea, "Why don't we throw him off a cliff into the river?" Now Terrapin knew that he was a great swimmer, but he wanted to pretend like that's not what he wanted, so he said, "Oh, no! No, don't do that! I'll drown if you do that." So the wolves thought this was the thing to do. So they took Terrapin and they threw him off the cliff, and he went down fast, and he was waiting to hit the water, but guess what? The river was so low at that time that he hits the rocks, and Terrapin's shell broke into a thousand pieces everywhere! As he was lying there, dying, Terrapin thought, "There's no way! No way on earth I'm ever going to be healed from this mess I'm in." But then something came to him. He remembered this song, this old, old song, and he started singing this song he remembered because it's a healing song.

He sings: "Whoaeh Yowah gonaway, whoaeh Yowah gonaway, whoaeh Yowah gonaway." While singing that healing song, he said, "I'm sewing myself back together. I'm sewing myself back together," and after a while, something miraculous happened. Some of those shell parts began to come back and form themselves on his back, but there were only thirteen of them, and they were just small little pieces. But sure enough, that song healed his back. Terrapin got up from there much smaller than he was before, and you know what? He walked a whole lot more humbly after that.

The Influence of the Western Worldview

Now that's the story of Terrapin and the wolves, and I thank my Chickamaugan friend Robert Francis for sharing that story with me. This is how I understand the Western worldview: it's Terrapin! It has taken up too much space, and it has insisted on its way in every single system that we have. In education, religion, economics, the criminal justice system, and politics. And that big Western worldview said, "We're doing this our way, 'cause we are right and everybody else has to come along or get run over. Do what we say or watch out!"

I also want to make an observation, which some may have made in hearing this story. Pedagogy is more important than content when we're teaching. It is ironic that this series is about Indigenous theology but is being delivered in a Western format. It is nobody's fault; it just is what it is. And that's why I have begun with stories, or narrative theology, if you will. I wanted to make this format more Indigenous, and for those educated in a Western system, it is more out of place. But story and conversation is Indigenized pedagogy.

The myth of progressive civilization is based on the Western worldview, displaying Greco-Roman and Anglo-Saxon White supremacy. Seneca wisdom-keeper and State University of New York–Buffalo professor John Mohawk states, "For the most part, contemporary historians have proceeded from the presumption that modern people are different from and superior to those who came before, especially those designated as primitives. Distortions and incomplete and even dishonest renderings of the past are found in many modern accounts of ancient and 'primitive' peoples. These accounts serve to reinforce the sense of difference and to distance moderns from unflattering legacies of the past."[11] In my opinion, John Mohawk was one of the greatest Native thinkers and writers to ever live, and he's from the Six Nations.

Where do these ideas about a just and right society come from, and how one civilization is better than the other? One of the myths that came along was how Greek civilization came about. If you do not think that the United States has been influenced by Greco-Roman civilization, all you have to do is go down to the nation's capital and see that every important building has great Greco-Roman pillars in front of it. Much of the capital city looks like buildings in Greece or Rome because they were influenced by the Renaissance. Here is another insight noted by John Mohawk: "Nineteenth-century German scholars seeking Arian roots for Western civilization promoted the idea

11. John C. Mohawk, *Utopian Legacies: A History of Conquest and Oppression in the Western World* (Santa Fe, NM: Clear Light, 2000), 260. See also Robert A. Williams, *Savage Anxieties: The Invention of Western Civilization* (New York: Palgrave Macmillan, 2012).

that Greek culture arose without antecedents, as if it metaphysically rose up from the hills of Greece. Like all other cultures however, Greek civilization was a product of time and place. It was not simply invented out of nothing. Greek culture inherited elements from earlier settlers in the area as well as from Mesopotamia and other civilizations around the Mediterranean."[12]

Every culture has an antecedent, or a learning time. There is no mythological instant grand culture whether Greece or, as we sometimes propose, the United States. Our North American Indigenous cultures did not arise out of nowhere. It took thousands of years for Indigenous peoples to develop our particular ethics and values. Those cultural shifts occurred through many ceremonies, many dreams, many revelations, and much wisdom over centuries and millennia, in order to come up with the values and ethics that are reflective of the land in which we all live. We, too, developed ancient ideas of democracy.[13]

Some believe democratic freedom in the United States is called to look like the House Freedom Caucus. That's what freedom is supposed to look like in the United States: white, male, corporate. This picture may be only slightly more diversified for Canada.

Understanding History and Our Place

I've garnered an education from a number of places over a number of years, with several books being foundational and

12. Mohawk, *Utopian Legacies*, 33.
13. Various forms of democratic governance were operating in a great many tribal nations before contact with Europeans. For example, the "Iroquois Influence Thesis" notes the influence of the Six Nations on the development of the US Constitution. It is posited that the democracy of the United States was influenced by the Iroquois model in the development of certain documents. The US Congress passed a resolution in October 1988 that specifically recognized the influence of the Iroquois League on the US Constitution and Bill of Rights.

which I commend: the first is *The History of White People* by
Nell Irvin Painter, who is a Black sociologist at Princeton. The
second, by a Native man, Robert Williams, is *Savage Anxieties:
The Invention of Western Civilization.* The third book is by a
Womanist theologian, Kelly Brown Douglas, who wrote *Stand
Your Ground: Black Bodies and the Justice of God.* Finally,
John Mohawk's *Utopian Legacies: The History of Conquest
and Oppression in the Western World.* These books really talk
about the history and rationale behind Greece and Rome and
then Anglo-Saxonism and will help all to understand our current history and civilization. How we understand history and
our place in it is important.

Through what lens did Jesus interpret history? We know he
interpreted history differently than a lot of the people around
him. We know this by passages like Luke 4:16–30:

> When he came to the village of Nazareth, his boyhood home,
> he went as usual to the synagogue on the Sabbath and stood
> up to read the Scriptures. The scroll of Isaiah the prophet was
> handed to him. He unrolled the scroll and found the place
> where this was written:
>
>> "The Spirit of the LORD is upon me,
>>   for he has anointed me to bring Good News to the
>>   poor.
>> He has sent me to proclaim that captives will be
>>   released,
>>   that the blind will see,
>> that the oppressed will be set free,
>>   and that the time of the LORD's favor has come."
>
> He rolled up the scroll, handed it back to the attendant, and
> sat down. All eyes in the synagogue looked at him intently.

Then he began to speak to them. "The Scripture you've just heard has been fulfilled this very day!" Everyone spoke well of him and was amazed by the gracious words that came from his lips. "How can this be?" they asked. "Isn't this Joseph's son?"

Then he said, "You will undoubtedly quote me this proverb: 'Physician, heal yourself'—meaning, 'Do miracles here in your hometown like those you did in Capernaum.' But I tell you the truth, no prophet is accepted in his own hometown.

"Certainly, there were many needy widows in Israel in Elijah's time, when the heavens were closed for three and a half years, and a severe famine devastated the land. Yet Elijah was not sent to any of them. He was sent instead to a foreigner—a widow of Zarephath in the land of Sidon. And many in Israel had leprosy in the time of the prophet Elisha, but the only one healed was Naaman, a Syrian."

When they heard this, the people in the synagogue were furious. Jumping up, they mobbed him and forced him to the edge of the hill on which the town was built. They intended to push him over the cliff, but he passed right through the crowd and went on his way.

They took him to the edge of the hill. They treated him like the wolves did Terrapin: "Let's throw him off the hill." But unlike Terrapin, Jesus was no bully, but his words did sting! The people of Nazareth were so upset because they had come to understand their own history differently than Jesus did.

Quite often early on in an anthropology course, students will hear the phrase, "I don't know who invented water, but it probably wasn't a fish." Sometimes we don't understand what we are all about, and it takes someone who has developed a different perspective to tell us what we are about. Obviously, those in the synagogue looked at their history differently than Jesus did. They understood their history and theology through an ethnocentric lens. But Jesus was reading scriptures like Amos 9:7 to understand his theology:

> "Are you Israelites more important to me
> than the Ethiopians?" asks the LORD.
> "I brought Israel out of Egypt,
> but I also brought the Philistines from Crete
> and led the Arameans out of Kir."

Jesus's theology was one that understood that God has a covenant relationship with all people.

"You Weren't Supposed to Learn This": Pre-colonization and America's History

In the remainder of this lecture I will talk about pre-colonization. In the second and third lectures, we will look more at the Western worldview. I'll focus on some specific aspects of it, particularly dualism. I'll also be looking at Indigenous theologies. Here is a brief precontact time line:

- Artifacts were found at Cooper's Ferry, Idaho, that dated from 16,500 years ago.
- Human hearths and charcoal dated to 13,500 BCE were found at Santa Rosa Island, California.
- Kodiak Island, where I spent two years, was occupied in 3500 BCE—that's about when Sumerians settled in Babylon.
- In 3372 BCE the Mayan calendar was made, which is more accurate than the Gregorian calendar.
- In 1200 BCE, the Olmec civilization existed, which is a pre-Aztecan group.

- In 753 BCE Rome was founded.
- In 1 CE the Hohokum built sites near the Salt River in the Sonoran Desert, creating an incredible system of irrigation.

How did First Nations in America travel here? This is where it gets controversial among our peoples because a lot of our people say, "We have always been here." And I am okay with that.[14] Our stories say that we were always here, but let's just say that you wanted to entertain the Beringia land bridge theory. This theory states that 13,000 to 17,000 years ago, we probably traveled on the kelp beds to get here from Asia and other parts of the world.[15] Over the years I have heard people theorize at least five entry points, including the Beringia land bridge theory.

In 1300 CE Native American populations are estimated to have been well over 65 million on the continent later known as North America. Some estimates are as high as 120 million.[16] In American schools we learn about ancient Greece, ancient China, and ancient Egypt. I learned about all those civilizations in school, but no one ever told me that my own people had advanced civilizations. I wonder why.

I have taught American church history twenty-one times in the past ten years, and I always begin with talking about pre-discovery—America before Columbus. I expand on some of the

---

14. See, for instance, Lynda Gray, *First Nations 101: Tons of Stuff You Need to Know about First Nations People* (Vancouver: Adaawx, 2011), 83.

15. Jon M. Erlandson, Michael H. Graham, Bruce J. Bourque, Debra Corbett, James A. Estes, and Robert S. Steneck, "The Kelp Highway Hypothesis: Marine Ecology, the Coastal Migration Theory, and the Peopling of the Americas," *The Journal of Island and Coastal Archaeology* 2 (2007): 161–74.

16. See Charles C. Mann, *1491: New Revelations of the Americas before Columbus* (New York: Knopf, 2005).

very things I have just outlined. In every single class it has never failed that someone asks, in one form or another, the same question: "Why didn't I learn about this in school?" These are master's-level students. I always give the same answer: "You weren't supposed to learn this."

So great civilizations were formed in the Americas, with unparalleled techniques in micro-agriculture, macro-environmental management, micro-ecology and macro-ecology, xeriscape, agronomy, botany, forestry, raised beds, and naturally self-sustained fertilized gardens. Sustainable architecture included passive solar, solar heating, water-capture systems, and mass water-transport systems. Humanities included psychology, philosophy, religion, theology, rhetoric, languages, the arts, and ethics. Sciences included math, medicine, surgery, brain surgery, dentistry, leeching poisonous foods to make them edible, healthy waste disposal, and urban planning. These civilizations also had democratic governments, education systems, intercontinental economic trade, complex peacemaking strategies, and more. All of these were already here, not everywhere, but they were present on the continent before any European ever set foot on these shores. These are advanced civilizations.

Ancient American civilizations were much healthier in many ways in their lifestyle, both personally and environmentally, and were more tolerant of diversity than Europeans. Look at our medicines. Even today, over five hundred medicines and herbal remedies are used in modern medical treatment that were first used by the First Peoples of the Americas—aspirin, quinine, and petroleum jelly, for instance. Sixty percent of the world's food eaten today originated in the Americas.

My wife and I have a small farm, and we also have a seed company for open-pollinated, mostly Indigenous seeds. If you like corn, potatoes, tomatoes, bell peppers, chili peppers,

vanilla, pecans, beans, pumpkins, cassava root, avocado, pea-
nuts, turkey, cashews, pineapple, blueberry, sunflower, wild rice,
chocolate, gourds, squash, many kinds of melons, sunchokes—
then be thankful for Native American civilization. All these
originated in the Americas.[17]

My people come from what we call "mound-building cultures." There are mound-building cultures in what is now Canada. I visited some of them near the Big Grassy Reserve in Ontario. These were large cities with large stadiums, palladiums,
gathering places, and homes. Mound-building cultures were
spread out from the Maritimes to the islands off Florida and
from western Ontario down through eastern North Dakota,
South Dakota, Nebraska, Kansas, Oklahoma, and Texas.

About the same time as Tutankhamun, the Hittite Empire,
Hammurabi, the Minoan civilization, Stonehenge, and the
Shang Dynasty, there was Poverty Point in present-day Loui-
siana, which is a UNESCO World Heritage Site. It was the
commercial trade and governmental center in its time. Poverty
Point had the largest and most elaborate earthworks anywhere
in the Western hemisphere. No other known earthen construc-
tions approached the size of Poverty Point until the nineteenth
century.

If you've visited the St. Louis area, in present-day Missouri,
all of ancient east St. Louis was a series of large cities, but only
one was saved. They call it Cahokia, and it's a ways outside the
city of St. Louis. Today, history tells us there was just one great
city called Cahokia, but Cahokia, as great as it was, was just

17. Emory Dean Keoke and Kay Marie Porterfield, *American Indian Contribu-
tions to the World: 15,000 Years of Inventions and Innovations* (New York: Check-
mark Books, 2003); Jack D. Forbes, *Columbus and Other Cannibals: The Wetiko
Disease of Exploitation, Imperialism, and Terrorism* (New York: Seven Stories, 2011);
Jack Weatherford, *Indian Givers: How Native Americans Transformed the World*
(New York: Three Rivers, 2010).

one of many in the area. Cahokia had about forty thousand people, but there were dozens of "Cahokias" nearby, and likely thousands of "Cahokias" among Native American mound-building cultures.

Chaco Canyon is one of those places that makes a lasting impression, and if one is interested they can see renditions online of what it may have looked like at one time between 900 CE and 1150 CE. Chaco Canyon was a major center of culture for ancient Pueblo peoples. By 1115 CE, it was connected to at least seventy-five outlying cities that had been built within the surrounding thirty thousand square miles. Composed of agricultural communities, trading posts, and ceremonial sites in the San Juan Basin, they were connected to one another by six major Chacoan roads. These main roads extended to at least another sixty roads, well-researched and surveyed, and generally straight routes that were lit up at night with signal fires. Chaco, like many ancient sites, also served as an astrological observatory.

The Hohokum (or as they are known now the Pima and Papago peoples) were living in the Sonoran Desert since circa 2000 BCE. They engineered remarkable things in the seventh through fourteenth centuries, including a complex series of canals, weirs, and irrigation networks with features of remarkable genius, rivaling the sophistication of those used in the ancient Near East, Egypt, and China. Casa Grande is a notable structure, and it served as an astrological observatory. Five hundred miles of canals irrigated over one hundred thousand acres in the driest land you can imagine. The scientific estimate is that the Sonoran Desert produced food with this advanced irrigation system that supported up to eighty thousand people. That would have been the highest population density in the prehistoric Southwest. The Phoenix metro areas continue to discover and reuse many of these ancient canals for similar purposes.

Where I live in the Pacific Northwest, there were several elaborate cultural notables, including the unique art and keeping track of sophisticated clan systems and relations. Scientists have figured out that the Pacific Northwest was probably considered the breadbasket of what we would call North America. Within a hundred miles of the Northwest coast was probably the most densely populated area on Turtle Island. A third of the Indigenous population of the Americas were located there and, if correct, that could mean between twenty and sixty million people.[18] A six-thousand-year-old record shows that up until the past two centuries, the Indigenous peoples of the Pacific Northwest never suffered from drought conditions.[19] Theirs were societies of abundance, not need. So what happened?

Discovery and Destruction

Churches have been talking about the Doctrine of Discovery now for some time.[20] This was the pope's decree that any Christian, king, prince, or nation could "discover" and assume dominion over lands previously known to non-Christians but unknown to Christians. But these lands were already inhabited. So here are some of the population estimates. Most of these come from Charles Mann's book *1491*.

18. See Kevin Starr, *California: A History* (New York: Modern Library, 2005), 13.
19. University of Pittsburgh, "6,000-year Climate Record Suggests Longer Droughts, Drier Climate for Pacific Northwest," *ScienceDaily*, February 23, 2011, www.sciencedaily.com/releases/2011/02/110222122725.htm.
20. For a recent treatment of the Doctrine of Discovery and its legacy in the United States, see Mark Charles and Soong-Chan Rah, *Unsettling Truths: The Ongoing, Dehumanizing Legacy of the Doctrine of Discovery* (Downers Grove, IL: InterVarsity, 2019).

What happened on this continent to cause such cataclysmic destruction? The first destructive wave was weather. You cannot win against weather. In about a 150-year period, approximately from 1125 to 1275 CE, America experienced several super droughts. Some estimate that as a result, there was up to a 50 percent population loss.[21] This period of ruin coincides with a number of places like Chaco Canyon, Cahokia Mounds, Okmulgee Mounds, Effigy Mounds, Gila Cliff Dwellings, Chichen Itza in Mexico, and others. When these cycles of drought began, these civilizations were at their height. These communities were densely populated, but even with good rains, the people were likely using their land to its limits. Without rain it was impossible to grow enough food to support the populations. Widespread famine occurred by the late 1300s. Most of the large Native American cities had all but died out and new patterns began emerging. That may be a lesson we have to learn again.

The second wave of devastation was disease. Disease was the unintended outcome of colonization. As much as 95 percent of the Indigenous people died almost immediately on contact with various European diseases, particularly smallpox. That calamity of infestation would have amounted to the decline of about one-fifth of the world's population, a level of destruction unequaled before or since. The stunning death rates of Native Americans who succumbed to European pathogens were due in part to lack of exposure but also to genetic traits that limited Native people's ability to deal with these unseen killers.

21. Pete Aleshire, "The Dry and Dusty Death of Civilizations: Studies Show Climate Shifts Have Played a Role in the Rise and Fall of Human Populations for 10,000 Years—and May Have Depopulated the Southwest," *Payson Roundup*, January 6, 2016, www.paysonroundup.com/outdoors/places_to_go/the-dry-and-dusty-death-of -civilizations/article_3b93b599-1fef-5e73-aa84-9eed4acec525.html.

Indigenous peoples are free of many genetic diseases but have a relatively narrow genetic range. American Indians have only about seventeen human-lycote antigens or HLAs, as opposed to Europeans who have, on average, thirty-five HLAs. HLAs are one of the human body's two main lines of defense against sickness. Helper t-cells are, in the case of Native Americans, oriented predominantly against parasites but are not as focused on bacteria and viruses as the immune systems of Europeans. Unfortunately, as a result of their clean-living standards and lack of exposure to pathogens of medieval Europe, the Native people in this land did not develop resistance to common European diseases such as mumps, measles, and chicken pox the way Europeans did. Because of infections like the Black Death or smallpox, we recognize today the wisdom and habits of personal cleanliness. The importance of good hygiene is a foundation of today's modern medicines. As a result of bathing in the same waters, entire groups would be wiped out by what are today preventable illnesses.

The European plagues that destroyed Native populations came in wave after wave, some plagues individually and others collectively, and had mortality rates as high as 95 percent. When we see these mortality rates, that likely means that several diseases came to them at the same time. These diseases were, for the most part, introduced incidentally, although at times with purposeful deliberation, but nearly always noted with celebration by the colonist. These plagues wreaked havoc on traditional Indian societies. Without realizing it, the Indigenous peoples met by the settlers were most often the traumatized and destitute survivors of ancient, advanced civilizations that had collapsed almost overnight.

Colonization and Christian Mission

The third wave of destruction was attempted genocide. In 1493 Christopher Columbus wrote to his patrons, "All these lands are densely populated with the best people under the sun. They have neither ill-will nor treachery."[22] Columbus recorded their generosity, and then he wrote about what a small military group it would take to overcome them and control them. These two people-groups inhabited two very different worldviews.

Anthropologist Carl Starkloff, in *The People of the Center*, notes,

> On reading the various accounts and monographs by explorers and anthropologists, what strikes one is the almost universal hospitality shown by Indian tribes, especially to their White visitors. It is quite remarkable as described in David Bushnell's writings about explorers and missionaries among the Siouan, Algonquian, and Caddoan tribes west of the Mississippi. . . . There are practically no examples of inhospitality or harsh treatment rendered to Whites. On the contrary, the tribal leaders went out of their way to receive these visitors as special guests. There seems to have been a conviction among the Indians, at least until the middle of the 19th century, that they and the newcomers could share the land equally, even if the land was sometimes thought to be the tribes' sacred inheritance.[23]

One of the early Pilgrim separatists was William Bradford, second governor of the Plymouth Colony. When Bradford discovered a whole Wampanoag village that had been wiped out,

22. Christopher Columbus, "Letter to the Sovereigns," March 4, 1493, University of California Press, https://publishing.cdlib.org/ucpressebooks/view?docId=ft009nb0cv&chunk.id=d0e5223&toc.depth=1&toc.id=&brand=ucpress, 192.

23. Carl Starkloff, *The People of the Center: American Indian Religion and Christianity* (New York: Seabury, 1974), 88.

he remarked, "The good hand of God favored our beginnings by sweeping away the great multitudes of Natives that he might make room for us."[24] His was a pretty typical attitude at the time. Christian mission was used as a colonizing strategy.

The 1637 massacre of a friendly Pequot village is described by leading Puritan theologian Cotton Mather: "Those that escaped the fire were slaine with the sword; some hewed to peeces, others rune throw with their rapiers. . . . It was a fearful sight to see them thus frying in the fryer and the streams of blood quenching the same, and horrible was the stincke and scent thereof, but the victory seemed a sweet sacrifice, and they gave the prayers thereof to God, who had wrought so wonderfully for them, thus to enclose their enemies in their hands."[25]

North America came to be by means of land theft, armed removal and relocation, forced breakup of families, the outlawing of Indigenous religion, bureaucratic policies of extermination, assimilation and racism, rape of the land—in other words, terrorism. Methods and policies may have changed over time, but intent did not. Our second former secretary of state, known as a statesman, was the politically compromising giant of statesmanship Henry Clay. He had this to say in 1825:

There was never a full-blooded Indian who took to civilization. It is not in their nature. They are destined to extinction. . . . I do not think they are, as a race, worth preserving. I consider them as essentially inferior to the Anglo-Saxon race which is now taking their place on this continent. They are not an improvable breed, and their disappearance from the human family will be no great loss to the world. In point of fact, they are

24. Quoted in Mann, *1491*, 56.
25. Quoted in Howard Zinn, *A People's History of the United States: 1492–Present* (New York: HarperCollins, 2003), 15.

rapidly disappearing and . . . in fifty years from this time there will not be any of them left.[26]

Clay's prophecy has proven untrue. For more than five centuries the Doctrine of Discovery and the international laws based on it, along with popular movements such as Manifest Destiny and American Exceptionalism, have legalized and rationalized the theft of land, labor, and resources from Indigenous peoples across the world and systemically denied their human rights. This is true in the whole of the Americas.

The Doctrine of Discovery originated with the Christian church and was based on the Christian scriptures, including the Great Commission (Matt. 28:18–20), Romans 13, and the narrative of a covenant people justified in taking land from the other as described in the Torah and the book of Joshua. The Doctrine of Discovery is still maintained in US law today.[27] Ethnic cleansing and genocide that occurred on elders, babies, families, tribal societies, civilizations, property—all of it created what we now call post-colonial stress disorder (PCSD). Native psychiatrists and psychologists are now stating that if you're a Native American, you likely have PCSD, post-traumatic stress disorder (PTSD), and intergenerational trauma as a result of the colonial plague.[28]

One example of this church-and-state collusion was a deliberate and strategic plan by both parties in the United States

26. Quoted in William G. McLoughlin, *Champions of the Cherokees: Evan and John B. Jones* (Princeton: Princeton University Press, 1990), vi.

27. See Robert J. Miller, *Native America, Discovered and Conquered: Thomas Jefferson, Lewis & Clark, and Manifest Destiny* (Westport, CN: Praeger, 2006).

28. See the following: Eduardo Duran and Bonnie Duran, *Native American Postcolonial Psychology*, Suny Series in Transpersonal and Humanistic Psychology (Albany: State University of New York Press, 1995); *Healing the Soul Wound: Trauma-Informed Counseling for Indigenous Communities*, 2nd ed., Multicultural Foundations of Psychology and Counseling (New York: Teachers College Press, 2019).

and Canada to create Indigenous people's poverty. It was pre-dominantly the church with the state's help in Canada, while in the United States it was the state with the church's help to create a planned dependency in spiritual matters, physical mat-ters, and economic matters. In the minds of many White folks, Indigenous people continue to be understood as either the poor Indian in need of rescue or as a vanishing race of noble savages to be admired from a distance. And yet we know that we can be fully self-empowering, self-sustaining, self-theologizing, and wise teachers to White society.

Racism and White Superiority

If we carry intergenerational trauma, then we also carry inter-generational wisdom. Perhaps it is in our genes and our DNA. But we continue to run into the same problems based on this myth of White superiority. We keep running into problems in colonized countries that show us that things have not actually changed that much. They just seem to happen less often. The United Nations Declaration on the Rights of Indigenous Peo-ples (UNDRIP) was finally accepted after generations by about 160 nations. But it is important to recognize who refused to sign: the United States, Canada, Australia, and New Zealand. The same four culprits who are not happy to accommodate Indigenous peoples. Eventually they signed.[29]

My family has experienced the hand of racism. We had created a center for empowerment for Native people on fifty acres in Kentucky. We had community, we had training, we

---

29. For a variety of discussions on UNDRIP in the context of the church, see Steve Heinrichs, ed., *Wrongs to Rights: How Churches Can Engage the United Nations Declaration on the Rights of Indigenous Peoples*, Intotemak (Altona, MB: Mennonite Church Canada, 2016).

had schools, we had Native elders living there and helping us, and it was empowering Native people. There's just something about a segment of the White population that can't stand to see Native people empowering themselves, and so a group of White supremacists came against us with a .50-caliber machine gun. They fired it day and night on our property line, and no one would help us. People who hear our story are like, "Oh, but those people in Kentucky are real rednecks." Perhaps, but the county sheriff would not help us. The state's attorney general would not help us. The Justice Department would not help us. Fair Housing Council would not help us. We were just a bunch of Indians to them. We were trying to empower ourselves, but apparently, being Indigenous is still a threat to White normalcy. In the end, we lost everything and had to begin again.

My friend Adrian Jacobs says it this way:

As in any recovery from debilitating socio-cultural problems the journey begins with, "Hello, my name is _____. I have a problem." . . . I am proposing that Aboriginal culture, world-view, frame of reference, and in this case, Aboriginal Christianity, offers hope to Western missionary autism. Aboriginal people are not your problem, we are your cure. . . . We are the conscience of your technology. We are the humanizers of your institutions. We matter, quite apart from your recognition of our worth. . . . We are a threat to entrenched powers-that-be who refuse to open the doors of opportunity and choice to all. We are a challenge to the mindset of greed, the avarice of Babylon, calling for the equitable distribution of resources in the spirit of the Jewish Year of Jubilee. We are good medicine for you.[30]

30. Adrian Jacobs, "Mitigating Missionary Autism: A Proposal for an Aboriginal Cure," *Journal of NAIITS* 9 (2011): 63, 70.

The Story of Grandmother Turtle

There's another Cherokee story about a turtle, but other tribal people have a similar story, and the story goes like this. Back in the old days, the animals were a whole lot bigger than they are now. They only lived on this one small place in Cherokee country. We call that place Blue Mountain. The animals came together and they were running out of room and they said, "You know, if we keep populating, we're not going to have any more room." And so they said, "Let's go to Creator and ask Creator to make more land for us and for our grandchildren's grandchildren." They knew Creator could do that and so they asked. But Creator thought, "Hmm, if I just make land for them, they won't be grateful for it. So, here's what I want you to do." So he says to the animals, "If you will send somebody down to the bottom of the water and grab some mud from the bottom of the water and come back up, I'll take that mud, and I'll spread it all over and make more land." So the animals said, "Okay. Sounds good."

Then all the animals gathered together in council, and they asked who would go get the mud. Right away Grandmother Turtle stood up, and she said, "I'll go get the mud." And no one wanted to be rude, but they also didn't want to wait for Grandmother Turtle since she was kind of slow and she was very old. So someone said, "How about Duck? Would you go get the mud?" And so Duck said she would. Mrs. Duck swam out a ways, took a big breath of air, and dived down into the water. Just a couple of seconds later Mrs. Duck popped back up. Then she dived down again, but she popped back up again! She did this a third time and she popped back up again. Mrs. Duck swam back to the shore, kind of embarrassed, and said, "You know, I'm a much better floater than I am a diver."

And so the animals say, "Okay, okay, well, who else can we send?" So right away Grandmother Turtle says, "I'll go get the mud." But this time they actually said aloud to Grandmother Turtle, "You know, Grandmother Turtle, we appreciate the offer but let's find somebody more qualified for such a difficult task." So the animals looked around and they thought, "Who's a good diver?" Then they saw Otter down the shore. Now Otter is an excellent diver and swimmer. And so they said, "Hey Otter. Would you go get the mud?" Right away Otter said, "Sure, I'll go get it!" Then Otter jumped in and took off. Otter was gone for one day, two days, and on the third day he came back, and they saw him down the beach a ways lying on his back. "What does he have in his hands?" someone asked. "Is it mud?" As they got closer to Otter, someone said, "He's eating a clam!" So they said to Otter, "Why are you eating a clam, and where's the mud we sent you after?" Otter said, "Well, you know I got going and I saw a fish and I started chasing it, and it took a while, and then I saw these clams, and, what was I after anyway?" Someone shouts in frustration, "Oh, you are no good to us, Otter!"

So now they wanted to find somebody serious who would go get the mud. Again, Grandmother Turtle stepped back up and she said, "I will go. I will get the mud." But this time the other animals just kind of crowded her outside the circle. Someone even said, "Grandmother Turtle, could you just be quiet back there? Let's find somebody who's really qualified." And so Beaver stepped forward. Beaver said, "You know what? I'm a good swimmer. I'm a good diver. I don't eat fish; you don't have to worry about that. And I work all the time, I don't play." So Beaver is gone all this time—she's gone for one day, two days, three days, and then the fourth day she comes back, and she says, "It's impossible. There's no way that anybody can get to the bottom and get the mud that's required." So they were all sad and complaining, but in the middle of their crying around and their sadness, Grandmother Turtle, without a word, slowly walked through the crowd and she slid down into the water and she was gone. Now, after what Beaver had said, they were afraid for Grandmother Turtle. But who else were they going to send? It seemed she was their last hope.

Grandmother Turtle was gone for three days with no sign of her. Then four days, and they're starting to get worried after the fourth day, so they put Squirrel up in the tree to keep a watch. And a fifth day goes by. The sixth day comes and goes but on the seventh day Squirrel yells out from the tree, "I think I see something. I see something coming up from the water." And they all looked out at the water. At first just a shiny reflection, but then, they saw it was Grandmother Turtle floating up to the top. Her legs were all out and limp as were her head and her tail. That's when they knew, Grandmother Turtle was dead.

They sent Duck and Beaver and Otter out to retrieve her, and they brought Grandmother Turtle back and laid her respectfully on the sand. Everyone was sitting around very sad, and they were crying because, you know, Grandmother Turtle gave her life for them. And they were sad because they had no way to have more land. It was a very gloomy day. The animals had no idea what to do as they were crying and talking to each other and comforting one another. Then someone said, "Hey! What's that in Grandmother Turtle's claw?" And they reached down, and they pulled her claws out, and in her hand, was this little ball of mud. So they took that ball of mud to Creator and they said, "Creator, here's the mud!"

What happened then was that Creator took that ball of mud and spread it all around and made what we today call Turtle Island, because if you look, North America is in the shape of a big turtle. Creator honored Grandmother Turtle's sacrifice by calling it Turtle Island. The animals were getting impatient for that mud to dry and so they said, "Hey, Grandpa Buzzard, why don't you go dry off the land?" And so Grandpa Buzzard started doing that. You know he was flapping his wings to dry it all and everywhere his wings went down, it created valleys, and everywhere his wings went up, it create mountains, and you know he was going across the mountains and then he got out to the plains, and somebody stopped him and said, "Hey, you know, Grandpa Buzzard, if you don't stop, there won't be any more flat land." So he just coasted for a while, and then he started back flapping.

Listening, Lamenting, and Memorializing

When I tell that story to little Native kids, do you know what the first thing they say is? Can you guess? They say, "They should have listened to Grandmother Turtle! She was the elder." Our Indigenous people have been here a long time. I see myself only as a predecessor to any and every Indigenous person from the territories you live in, whom you will invite to your places and to your organizations, to share wisdom with you and to be asked to be on every committee you have. They are your Grandmother Turtles. You should listen. I'm here, hopefully opening the door or continuing to open the door for those host Indigenous people to help you on your land and to help you with your worldview. In the next two lectures I will be talking about our worldviews.

It never fails that someone asks right away, "What can we do?" And that's always a question on European minds. European minds first want to know and then they immediately want to fix it, quickly. They believe they can fix everything; this is part of the worldview. I want to preempt that presumptive question. Usually, the answer I give is just to listen for a long time. That part is crucial. But after you're done listening for a long time, here is a little paradigm to begin working through. First, what White Western folks must do, both structurally and individually, is to heal the relationships between themselves, Creator, the land, and the local Indigenous peoples. It starts with awareness; it is exactly what you are doing in reading this. An education process led by Indigenous people but done on their terms and in their comfort zone. So what you may want to do is not necessarily to ask the Indigenous people of this land to come here, but you should go to where they are, and be sure you pay them well because, most times, we don't get paid well. Settler White people often feel like it is the responsibility of Indigenous people to educate them and to do it gratis.

Second, we need to lament together because that is part of becoming a community. Confession in the public square, speaking truth to power.[31] Allow time for it to sink in and then, very importantly, reparations need to be made. I prefer to call reparations "rehumanizing." Restitution first, because invariably, that is the last thing that ever gets done or it is the one thing that never actually gets done. But reparations are exactly the thing that helps Western folks to take the process and the relationship seriously. What happens when settler folk make reparations to Indigenous people? Quite a while ago Dan Rather, one of our great news reporters, was interviewing Mother Teresa, and Dan decided to ask her a theological question. He said, "Mother Teresa, why did Jesus say the poor will always be with us?" And she looked at him kind of funny,

31. See Anna Robbins, "No Reconciliation without Repentance: Accepting Collective Responsibility for Historical Sin," *Journal of NAIITS* 13 (2015): 119–34.

and she said, "Well, that's easy. If the poor are not with us, the rich can't be saved." Like Zacchaeus, reparations are the settler's opportunity to be saved/healed (Luke 19:8–9).

Finally, memorializing is important. Working together in partnership, retelling history, codifying the markers. It's interesting that so often in the Old Testament you see when a great thing happens in ancient Israel's history, marker stones are put down to memorialize those things so that future generations will know what happened there (Gen. 31:45–46; 35:14; Josh. 4:3–10). Memorials are intended to restore relationships of the past for future generations, which means looking back to go forward. You should be asking yourselves, "What were the original relationships supposed to be with the Creator, the land, and the Indigenous people of this area?" This requires a new paradigm based on re-empowering the host authority of Indigenous people of the land. It may not always mean tribal governments; it may mean other agencies, so you must be open, constantly in the process of decolonizing the Western worldview of settler colonialism and re-Indigenizing. Think in terms of the local and regional watershed, not the colonial grid pattern.[32] Think about Indigenous perspectives and values, and ask the questions, How does this speak to the faith question? How does it speak to churches? How does it speak to politics? How does it speak to education? How does it speak to our economic systems? What is brought from the European tribes that could remain intact, and what should be discarded at this time?

---

32. See Ched Myers, ed., *Watershed Discipleship: Reinhabiting Bioregional Faith and Practice* (Eugene, OR: Cascade Books, 2016).

I've heard the saying, "Christianity is a White religion," suggesting why some Indigenous people have rejected Christianity. What are your thoughts on this?

Perhaps "*some* have rejected Christianity" is an understatement. First of all, realize, it's an interesting dilemma, especially for those of us who have a relationship with Jesus and have grown further into our Indigeneity while continuing to follow Jesus. There's always those who walk away at that point and maybe that's something they need to go through. But if you're following Christianity and asking, "Is Christianity compatible with Indigenous values?" I would say, well, it depends what history you read on what day. I'm not sure that Christianity *is* compatible with Indigenous values, but I'm pretty certain that following Jesus seems to be. If you're more interested in following Jesus than following Christianity, I don't think there's a conflict.

How would you differentiate Christianity from following Jesus?

I think what we do, and this part pertains to our worldview, is to pick and choose the parts of Christianity that we like. We all have bad actors in our families, right, that we, well, maybe don't put them up front right away? But if we take the whole of the religion and we study it honestly, we understand that Christianity basically married empire with the Emperor Constantine and has never been able to separate itself from empire ever since. So it doesn't mean that Christians can't follow Jesus, but I say it this way: you *can* be a Christian and follow Jesus, but it's very difficult.

You mentioned the Great Commission and how that's connected with colonization. Can you tell us how you think followers of Jesus should read the Great Commission?

What I mentioned was in reference to the Doctrine of Discovery. Matthew 28:18–20 is one of many scriptures that have been used to trample over the rights of Indigenous people and others. At one point in my life, I was what you might call a "flaming evangelist." Many of you may have heard of the Billy Graham KNOCK program, or the Two Question Test with Glad Tidings School of Evangelism, or the Four Spiritual Laws, or Evangelism Explosion. I was trained in all of those when I was a younger person. I was evangelizing at malls and at Jesus festivals, and I was on the streets witnessing at 3:00 a.m. to pimps and prostitutes. I was the man leading people to Jesus. But I always had this sinking feeling inside when I was evangelizing. I felt that there was something wrong with what I was doing but could not put my finger on it. I am witnessing, which is what they told me to do. They told me, bottom line, that following Jesus just means to go out and get other people to follow Jesus. Well, there was a whole lot of in-between that I was missing, and one of the things I was missing was that I was treating people as objects of my agenda. I had no concern for their person compared to my concern for their "soul." I was operating in a very dualistic way, and it felt very unnatural. So I began to wrestle with that, and one of the things I did was to realize I needed help understanding all this "whole gospel" stuff, so I began to seek out different places and different people to help give me a more balanced view.

It was during that time when someone asked me, "Why don't you just interpret scripture through your Indigenous eyes?" I was kind of offended at that, and I didn't get it right away, but I eventually realized that Jesus was not an Enlightenment-bound thinker. Jesus was an Indigenous man. In fact, none of the scriptures were written from an Enlightenment view, but they were taught to me that way. So I began to understand the scriptures differently and more importantly, I began to understand Jesus differently.

Concerning evangelism, I began to understand that this precious moment when a person decides to follow Jesus is a very sacred time. To treat people as an object of my own agenda or to disregard any part of their life is really not treating that person as a sacred human being, but is disrespectful. That was the unease I felt inside. I had to rethink that whole process, and my understanding now is that it's not that that scripture is no good or doesn't count, but that love includes respect for the other person's dignity. How I go about doing that now is with great respect for the person's dignity. This type of encounter is very different now than it was at one point in my life.

How ought we to read the exodus story?

How I understand the exodus story is that it was written a good number of years after the surrounding history happened, and it was written for a particular reason—namely, it appears, to drum up nationalism among Israel. To this date, there's still no archaeological support that it actually happened. So what I understand from what we know about it, is that the scripture is teaching me, this is what can happen when you depart from Jesus and move into extreme nationalism. So what's written is true, and that's the truth of it that I understand.

I'll talk more about the differences in understanding story in the next lecture, but I'll say this now: I used to use a little pie chart that shows 75 percent of the scriptures are narrative or story as we say. My Old Testament professor colleagues tell me that it's really more like 90 percent of the scriptures are narrative. So, how we understand narrative is really very important if we want to understand the scriptures. Where you end up really comes down to how you understand narrative, and currently, the modern Western worldview says, narrative is fact, and fact equals truth. Indigenous worldviews might say that we understand narrative has truth, and facts are, well, not so important as truth.

When we hear stories in church, it's to illustrate a point. Sermon stories tend to have a funny punch line, but stories are used in a different way with Indigenous pedagogy.

Yes. Among my Keetoowah people and much of the tribal peoples in the Southeastern United States, we are part of what we call stomp dance culture. That's our religion. It comes from the Sun, which is the most visible thing that we can see, and some of us think of the Creator as being behind the Sun; Creator is the one behind everything, and the Sun is a representation of all that. In the so-called "Sun Cult" tribes you'll see a lot of pottery with this (and in my own tattoos). But you would see that Sun symbol, the ancient Sun symbol and then our fire, which represents God as the incarnation of God coming down to earth.

As God's presence comes down on earth, we dance around that fire all night and we sing songs, and we have what's called a preacher who gives a message. Not an ordained Christian preacher, but our spiritual leaders, but they're just called the preacher. They stand around the fire, and they talk to the people, each one sitting with their different clans. They teach and preach by telling stories. Those stories tell us how to live: they talk about our ethics, our worldview, the values that we're supposed to have, how we're supposed to treat other people and treat the earth. The stories around the fire are the main event. But the Western world is short on stories.

The story in the Western world is the thing you tell as the concluding point, or the children's moment in some traditions. But people love to hear stories; in stories, we find ourselves because we relate to our humanness. I prefer to tell stories in a different setting than this. If I were in charge of organizing a time of teaching and it was done in my "comfort zone," we would all be sitting around the fire, and I'd be walking around talking to you by that fire, and I would mostly tell stories.

Could you explain to us "Creator" from an Indigenous perspective?

I can't speak for anyone other than myself, but I don't know what being a "king" really is in the world. Creator is Creator. Creator is the being from which everything that exists comes to be, as it says in Colossians 1. Creator holds everything together, and so I understand my role as a human being to be one who keeps harmony among all of these things on earth and sky and under the earth and in the water, and among other humans. So, Creator to me is in everything. In my own theological development, what I understand, and it's pretty clear in the scriptures, is that Jesus is Creator (John 1:1–14). John 1:3 says, "God created everything through him [Jesus], / and nothing was created except through him."

Colossians 1:17 and following states not only that he created everything that exists in the world but that he continues to hold everything together (cf. 1 Cor. 8:6). The writers of the

New Testament didn't know what to do with Jesus. How do you explain the experience of Creator becoming human flesh? They said he was with God and he is Creator, having what we call the "efficacy" of creation. And so, for me, when I pray to Creator, and how I understand my people have been praying to Creator, I understand that they are and have been praying to Jesus. Maybe they don't want to look at it that way, and that's okay. In my mind, they're still praying to Jesus. He is the Creator.

This is not something the West has really relished talking about for some reason. Jesus exists in the perfect community—what I call the Community of Creator. And perfect shalom is the preference and deference for one another in this unity and diversity, which has its mark on all creation. Of everything created, there is nothing singular in the whole universe (or multiverse if there is such a thing) or no matter how far down you go. You can keep going and you keep going and you keep going until you get down to a cell, and then you keep going and then you get down to the atom. And you keep going and you break the atom down to its parts and then, finally, on the subatomic level, you see this unity and diversity of the Community of Creator reflected in these tiny things called quarks.

A group of scientists won the Nobel Prize a number of years ago for increasing our understanding of quarks. They didn't discover quarks because other scientists already knew they were there, but knowledge of them was limited. Quarks are these little colored lights inside the atom, and the strange thing about them is they change colors and they move around, but they're never single. They always form in groups. Maybe at one time there's a group of three along with another group of ten and another of six and then they switch around in various groupings but never just one alone. Nothing singular, because

Creator's DNA, Creator's fingerprint, is unity and diversity. Sometimes humans are the last ones to figure that out.

What do you do when you hear a rebuttal that mentions the one or two instances where Indigenous peoples did something bad to themselves or bad to the environment?
This type of rebuttal contains within it the inherent problem of assumed equivalency. Sometimes, because of binary thinking, it comes down to "Well, we're good and you're bad," when the truth is that none of us are all good or all bad, and none of our societies were all good or all bad. But hopefully we're all working through stuff, and even then we still don't get it right every time. And here's the assumed equivalency. Our Indigenous cultures have been here for tens of thousands of years, and there have been lots of times when we didn't get it right. But we've been learning on this continent longer than anyone else. So I think we've gotten more correct and more often, and so have more wisdom to share.

When you think about the way that scripture arrived in North America through settler colonialism and on the back of disease and wave after wave of death, does that affect how you see the value of scripture versus the value of a kind of general revelation among Indigenous peoples?
So, how could we believe the scriptures after all this has happened, including with all the baggage that comes with Christianity? For me, the first point is, I'm different from most of my Indigenous friends. Of the people I hang with, I'm of the minority opinion that I don't believe the scriptures should have ever been written or translated for our people. We already had our own way of knowing stories. We already had our own epistemologies, and they were probably more accurate, and so, the stories should have

been told, and we would have learned the stories. I believe the Word of God is not the Bible but the stories held within it and Jesus, of course, who is the Word of God (John 1:1).

Second, I would say that I've only met three Native atheists in my whole life, and all three people had to work hard at it to get there. Two of them learned it in universities, but they also had never spent time with any traditional person. I've spent time with a lot of different traditional people from a lot of different traditions over the years. Many believe Jesus was great, but they think kind of like Gandhi, who was purported to have said, "It's the Christians that I have trouble with, not Jesus."

This is a complicated response, complicated because I see two layers of traditional people. And forgive me if I offend anybody, but my wife and I were both really fortunate to be able to be around older elders, very old elders who understood themselves well and who were generous to a fault. They had so much grace, much more than I do. When I try to talk about these things, I think of the various elders, family, and others. I think, *What would they say?* or *What would they want me to say?* But then, we have a sort of new class of folks, and I call these ones neo-traditional. And they don't often have a lot of forbearance. And they don't often have a lot of tolerance. And they tend to get angry easily.

There's nothing wrong with anger, by the way, but in this other, older traditional group of people that I'm talking about, I never met anyone who didn't have tolerance or grace for anyone who wanted to follow Jesus, because each person has to work out spirituality themselves, and they had so much patience for that.[33] Even after experiencing so much trial and

33. On the sacredness of the individual's pursuit of spirituality, see Charles A. Eastman Ohiyesa, *The Soul of the Indian* (1911; repr., n.p.: Digital Scanning, Inc., 2001).

anguish, still they were so forgiving. They can forgive all the bad. But that does not mean that we ignore the bad. It just means that you can forgive it and realize that we're all human beings, we all make mistakes.

Our family traveled all across the United States and Canada for so many years, and there's one sort of message that we would come across in sweat lodges and at other reserves and places. In many places, the message was something like, "Creator, when you look down on me, have pity, because I'm just a human being." That seems to be one of our greatest theological statements—we're just human beings, and so we also can forgive other human beings. If we were perfect, we wouldn't need Creator. So we're all just being human and being vulnerable, which to me is the most human thing you can be. I consider Creator to be the most vulnerable being who exists, and it is in my vulnerability that I exhibit my spirituality, my humanity. So being human is a good thing. I guess the simple answer to that question is that we are all just human, and so we must continue to work together.

2

Comparing Western and Indigenous Worldviews

A Proper Introduction

Chief Seattle stated:

> Every part of the soil is sacred in the estimation of my people. Every hillside, every valley, every plain and grove, has been hallowed by some sad or happy event in days long vanished. Even the rocks, which seem to be dumb and dead, as they swelter in the sun along the silent shore, thrill with memories of stirring events connected with the lives of my people, and the very dust upon which you now stand responds more lovingly to their footsteps than yours, because it is rich with the blood of our ancestors, and our bare feet are conscious of the sympathetic touch.[1]

Chief Seattle did not speak these words because he wanted to say, "We're better than White folks." He observed this because

1. Authentic text of Chief Seattle's Treaty Oration—1854. Originally published in the *Seattle Sunday Star*, October 29, 1887.

of the way that the settler folks treated the land and the way they looked at the land. I suggest that he meant that the land hasn't welcomed settler folk because the settlers have not bothered to ask to be welcomed to the land. No proper introduction with the land was sought. Instead, they were presuming that it was theirs for the taking. This is, in my opinion, the most authentic text that he spoke, and I want to suggest that it is not too late to be introduced properly to the land.

There is a story that I want to share from Cherokee country. This is a story about a time when our Cherokee people were actually misusing the land, misusing the animals, and misusing the plants. As the story goes, our people began to take for granted the food sources they had. They would kill animals indiscriminately and just take the best parts of the meat, and leave the rest to rot. So the animals got tired of this and held a council. In that council, the animals got together and said, "We've got to do something about this! We have got to stop these Cherokee people from doing what they're doing." So they asked one another, "How are we going to do it?"

The Bears were the first to step forward, and they said, "Well, we're going to be in charge of this problem; we'll help you figure it out, and we'll all come up with something." (This is kind of an inside joke because in the Cherokee way, the Bears are our closest relatives, so they're the closest to being human. Now you can understand why the Bears are going to take charge of everything.)

So, one Bear asked, "How are they killing us?" Several animals spoke up and replied, "They're killing us with bows and arrows." "Okay," said Bear, "let's make bows and arrows and kill them too!" So they fashioned bows and arrows, and they went to practice with those bows and arrows. As you know, bears have long claws that got in their way, so they never could hit anything with those bows and arrows. Arrows were flying all over the place and rabbits were jolting and squirrels were scurrying just to avoid getting hit. Finally, one Bear admitted, "Look, you know this is not going to work very well for us. We're going to have to cut off our claws to shoot straight, and, you know, we make our living with our claws. So, you know, we dig for grubs and we are digging on the ground and things, and so I don't think that's going to work out." By this time the rest of the animals in the council said, "You know what, Bears, you had your chance, and you blew it. Let's find someone else to sort of lead the discussion here." So they elected Inchworm.

Inchworm sat on a log and got input from everyone. As the animals began to share, Inchworm started speaking: "As you were all talking, I had an idea." So, Inchworm asked, "What if we put disease on the people? What if we put disease on those Cherokee and we get our revenge that way?" And so, they start thinking about that and they all decided, "Yeah, that's a good way to get them. Let's think of some diseases." And so, they thought of smallpox and they thought of chicken pox and influenza and scarlet fever and polio and all the sorts of plagues and different things that they put on them.

The Cherokee people began to die. First the young children began to die and then the old people, then the men began to die, and then even the strong women began to die. The tribe at that point knew that they wouldn't exist anymore if they didn't do something about it. So they went to the animal council and they said, "Look, please, we know what we were doing was wrong, but we want to apologize, and we want you to forgive us and take these diseases away." But the animals said, "Nope, we're not going to do it." They decided to be stubborn about it, so the Cherokee people continued to die. Now, all this time the plant people were watching this, and the plants held a council too.

The plants all said, "You know, we feel sorry for those Cherokee. They're sorry for what they have done. I think we can teach them now." And so the plants decided that they would start coming to the Cherokee people in their dreams, and one would come in a dream and say, "Here's the plant you use to take care of this disease." And another, "Here is the plant you use to take care of this disease, and here's how you use it." Pretty soon, the Cherokee people began to heal themselves with the medicines that the plants gave them.

Finally, it came about that all three groups got together—the animals, the plants, and the Cherokee people—and they decided what they would do to cooperate together. From now on, if a Cherokee hunter went out looking for food for his family, he would first pray a prayer and sing a song asking that the animal would give itself up to him. And if the animal didn't give itself up to him, then he wouldn't kill the animal. But, if he did kill the animal, the first thing he would do is he would thank that animal, and then he would put some tobacco down on the ground and thank the earth, and then he would pray and thank Creator for providing all of this.

And things went the same way with the plants. The plants decided that would be a good way for human beings to understand that when they take something out of the earth, they had to give something back. So if you put down tobacco and remind yourself that you're taking something from the earth, and you are putting something sacred back, then you would never take advantage of that or take it for granted. And so that's the way things went from that point on, and our elders even today will tell us that for every disease, there's a plant cure. Those plants sometimes still come to us in our dreams, and the plants talk to us in our dreams.

As you hear this story and reflect, what do you hear? Depending on the person and their experiences, different things will be heard in that story. Some recognize the connection between everything, the symbiotic relationship between everything, each having a measure of dependence on the other. Other hearers will identify the level of respect and acknowledgment between all of the beings, and the rights of each. Others are struck by the dialogue between the species. This is not something we care as much about these days, talking to and listening to plants and animals (Job 12:7–10). Keep this story in mind as we move through the lecture, because that story is really the basis of all that follows.

Creation and Creator

When I look at the Genesis passages through my own cultural lens, I find a lot of similarities to Indigenous stories like this one. In the Genesis accounts of creation, I find a world where each part of creation is related to the other. When God makes the first human and I anticipate what will happen next, I see the requirement for Adam to name all the animals. But to name things in an Indigenous way, you have to get to know them, and to know their special characteristics. In the narrative, God is telling Adam to go out and get to know his relatives. The creation narratives in Genesis, like many Indigenous creation narratives, encourage humans to see the wider created order as part of the same "family tree of the heavens and the earth" (Gen. 2:4).[2]

2. On this translation and relational understanding, see H. Daniel Zacharias, "The Land Takes Care of Us: Recovering Creator's Relational Design," in *The Land: Majority World and Minoritized Theologies of Land*, ed. K. K. Yeo and Gene L. Green (Eugene, OR: Cascade Books, 2020), 77–80.

The importance of the narrative is that it is not just about humans. It is also about the animal kingdom and the plants and the water and the sky and everything else. We tend to take that for granted, but I think the original stories are meant to help us see a bigger picture than what we normally see. My theology begins with the land. I can pretty much find any kind of belief system or understanding I have and trace it back to the land. I've been criticized for this. People will say, "My theology begins with the Creator." My response to this is, "What do you stand on in order to talk to the Creator?"

If you don't have land (including the water), you can't talk to Creator. Creator gave you land and wants you to know it. So, my understanding is that our responsibility as Indigenous people is to be keepers of the land. That means the whole of all the ecosystems and all the human systems. Our role is to maintain harmony and balance. That is my job on earth. That is the job I take seriously while I'm here. When the land is used badly, and the community of creation is mistreated, everything becomes out of balance and in disharmony. Anywhere on earth can be a place of harmony when you understand your role, but it's not utopia; there's a difference.

I want readers to think about some foundational questions about land, story, and social location. Who is God to us? I am reminded of the story of Ganesh and Kartikeya, the famous race around the world that was to take place. Ganesh is the Indian god; the elephant-looking Indian god, and he and his brother (or her brother, as Ganesh is sometimes referred to as female) were going to race. Kartikeya challenged Ganesh to a race three times around the world. Kartikeya took off as fast as possible, but Ganesh just found his parents and walked around them three times and said, "I've won, declare me the winner." But his parents said, "No, you have to go around the world three times." But Ganesh said, "You are my world." Our reality really depends on our perspective! The world, or my world—who gets to decide?

Who Gets to Decide Which Perspective Wins?

This is the question that we might be asking ourselves in this period of time: "Who gets to decide which perspective wins?" We have the story of Adam and Eve from the Hebrew Bible, and many people would say we are all children of Adam and Eve. I myself, I am a child of Selu and Kanati. Selu and Kanati are the first man and woman in our Cherokee stories. Selu is the corn-woman, and in our story, she was created first, not Kanati the hunter. How do I know that I'm a child of Selu and Kanati? I know because when I hunt, I pray and sing before I go out, and then I wait. If an animal doesn't give itself to me, I don't take it. I am a son of Kanati, the hunter. Also, I plant corn every year; I'm a son of Selu, corn-woman, corn-mother. Corn feeds our family. The Cherokee corn I plant is sometimes up to 20 percent protein. This is one of the reasons that we continue to have a seed company, because we think it is important to preserve and continue these seeds that were so valuable at one point to our people and can still be valuable to us now.

I'm a son of Selu and Kanati because I continue the ceremonies that go along with those stories, and I continue telling the stories of my people, and those stories exhibit our values, and those stories exhibit our ethics, and those stories tell us about our identity. They tell us how to live in the world. And for some, that is the point of Adam and Eve.

Back to the question, most often those in power get to decide. But God is more powerful through our faith, which is perhaps the crux of the Christian faith, and the point of the gospel story. That is to say, our faith is the protest that Christians are called to live into, and against, the illegitimate powers of this world—that which destroys harmony. So that's how I understand my role as a Jesus-follower too. It is to continue to bring balance or bring harmony to a broken and fragmented society. That works well with what I understand my "marching orders" from Jesus to be. So we are to stand up against the illegitimate powers of this world and those things that would disrupt harmony. I once heard an interview with John Mohawk where he stated something like, "I think we need to study Western civilization in order to understand when certain narrow and limiting thinking first appeared and where we went wrong." Throughout his book *Utopian Legacies*, he hammers on the utopian societies from the Greco-Roman world, forward to now in the Americas. Utopianism almost always ends up deciding that the ends justify the means. Anything can be done, and has been done, to justify the ends in utopian societies. The idea being that if you believe strongly enough, then you'll do what you feel is necessary. Colonization is a result of utopianism in that colonization brings rootless urbanization. Rootless urbanization has no consciousness of specific place. This results in universalizing theologies and ideas and philosophies. Once you have a utopian vision set in place, anything that goes against that can be rationalized as evil.

In the colonial vision, there's a "greater good" that had to result in a war on Indigenous peoples. Problematizing Indigenous peoples was, in a way, a war on place. A war against both the specific land and the idea of place. This universalizing theory says everything is universal, everything is abstract, nature is abstract and therefore, what I do or say in Philadelphia, I can do in San Francisco or I can do in Halifax or I can do in Vancouver—it doesn't matter because it is universalized. Local place, and everything that has occurred there prior to colonization, has no meaning for the present and future. Place is simply the same everywhere one goes. This is the colonization of place. We have perfected this in the United States. We call it the American dream. We have created this utopianism based on wealth where everybody can get wealthy, and it doesn't matter what you have to do to the people or the land to achieve this dream.

Western Religion and Indigenous Theology

So, who is God to us? The answer to the question depends not just on what we think but on how we think. Generally, Indigenous folks understand ourselves as part of the land. We understand ourselves as primarily communal, and this is inclusive of land.[3] We understand truth through narrative and instinctively find our place in the story and we activate toward that truth. Generally, Western folks understand themselves apart from or distinct from the land. They understand themselves primarily individually. They understand truth through facts and propositions. They instinctively separate themselves from the story for "objectivity's" sake and they divide reality.

My sixty-three years of experience in America have taught me that beliefs are basically everything to Western folks and the practices and values in the worldview are just a part of that, but not a big part of it. In an Indigenous worldview, all of life is spirituality, beliefs are de-emphasized, spirituality is passed on primarily via observation and participation or practices. Correct practices show beliefs and reaffirm values and worldview.

3. Ray Aldred, "The Land, Treaty, and Spirituality: Communal Identity Inclusive of Land," *Journal of NAIITS* 18 (2019): 1–17.

Knowledge is what one has lived and experienced, but for the
Euro-American reality, religion is just a part of life and beliefs
are overly emphasized.

In the Western worldview, religion is passed on primarily via
correct doctrine or orthodoxy. Correct doctrine shows beliefs:
knowledge is learned, and information or facts are what matter. Characteristics of Indigenous theology and practice have
a creation-based theological foundation that emphasizes harmony and balance, being centered, and seeking cooperation.
Indigenous theology is fundamentally holistic, has a common
spirituality, is specific to a group, and is a theology of place
over time. There are stark differences between the two. You can
see now how important it was to have the blessing of the Indigenous people here at the beginning of the event. They were
given the honor due that allows them to decide what happens
on this land. They are the keepers of this particular land.

Indigenous narrative theology is ceremonially centered with a
localized theology, with local polity, expressed in various forms
of mutuality, with an immanent, present-centered Christology
where the Creator-Son being is a construct. There's a relational
trinity in Indigenous thinking. Euro-American theology and
practice is redemption based, modern, about conquest—it seeks
to rule over nature, and it's fundamentally fragmentary.

European theology has a Father theological concept, a positional Trinity, and vicarious participation, leading to reflection
and affirmation. Now, comparing these, I call Native American
religious reality "epistemological orthopraxy," where truth
comes by understanding how others have lived. This is mainly
taught through story. Through this understanding we learn
how we are to live. Truth is intimately related to experience;
words have primordial power when spoken. The spirit of verbal
story is not doctrine; it is ceremony and tradition.

In the Indigenous way, explanation actually weakens the power of words and makes them less true. Writing words makes them lose power.[4] A circular worldview of harmony and balance seeks to reconcile via integration, accommodation, and negotiation. A Western, Euro-American worldview is what I call "epistemological orthodoxy." Truth comes by learning what others have believed. This comes mainly through doctrine, law, and such things. By learning these things, one knows how to live, but truth may be unrelated to experience, and words have power only when written; spoken words mean little, whereas written word is doctrine or truth. Story is for illustration of truth. Writing words seems to make them truer in the Western worldview and strengthens their power. The linear worldview of conquest seeks to resolve through conflict, overtaking the opponent through words, physical aggression, and winning. Losing strategies create an either-or option as the primary solution.

This is seen through the law of noncontradiction in Christianity and the West. One is saved or lost, goes to heaven or hell, has correct doctrine or is heretical. It's a win or lose proposition. No room for mystery or nuance or even non-certitude or humility. An example of a conquest worldview might lead to a value of superiority and a practice of racism, classism, sexism, and similar things. Even though the stated belief is equality in leadership, the practice might be hierarchical leadership. But Indigenous peoples learn naturally from our childhood forward that all things are related to one another. It takes superficial learning to create and maintain artificial categories of reality. In time, these categories become realities.

Disintegration occurred in the West as a result of dualism between such areas as mind and flesh, spirit and body, material

4. See Ray Aldred, "The Resurrection of Story," *Journal of NAIITS* 2 (2004): 5–14.

and ethereal. The disintegrated worldview has the advantage of being able to concentrate in depth on one category or on specifics, but its deficit is the missing relationship of the real categories. Western theology tends to be abstract and dualistic and coupled with power, resulting in a theology that has been applied universally and normalized in the West. This is theological hegemony.

We must ask ourselves, In what ways has Western Christian theology been universalized and normalized, not just in content but also in epistemology, pedagogy, and practice (or lack of praxis), and in what ways has it been dualistic? Here is an example: John Winthrop, who is one of our founders in the early Boston Colony and who was the second governor of the Boston Colony, made a "legal declaration," annulling any Native claims to the land. The Indians, he said, "had not subdued the land and therefore had only a natural right to it, but not a civil right to it."[5]

A natural right did not have legal standing, and this was a way of creating a law that lawfully steals land. I'm reminded of Deuteronomy 27:17: "Cursed is anyone who steals property from a neighbor by moving a boundary marker." Dualism in Christian mission was used as a colonizing strategy. Relegating Indigenous theology to its current social location, Cotton Mather, in his book *Magnalia Christi Americana*, said this of the Pequot Massacre: "In a little more than one hour, five or six hundred of these barbarians were dismissed from a world that was burdened with them."[6] Regarding the same event, Captain John Underhill stated, "It may be demanded, should

---

5. Howard Zinn, *A People's History of the United States: 1492–Present* (New York: HarperCollins, 2003), 14.
6. Cotton Mather, *Magnalia Christi Americana*, vol. 2 (1702; repr., Bedford, MA: Applewood Books, 2009), 482.

not Christians have more mercy and compassion? But I would refer you to David's war. Sometimes the scripture declareth women and children must perish with their parents. We had sufficient light from the word of God for our proceedings."[7]

Colonial religion, according to the Western mind, brings future hope. The promises of Western Christianity include our salvation, development, security, and civilization. But what is actually delivered to Indigenous peoples is imbalance, oppression, violence, and destruction. The land is destroyed as it is consumed. This conquest mentality has been written about by anthropologists and sociologists and others for a number of years. One anthropological study by Arensberg and Niehoff stated, "This conquering attitude towards nature appears to rest on at least three assumptions: that the universe is mechanistic, that [humankind] is the master and that [humankind] is qualitatively different from all other forms of life. . . . Specifically American and Western [humankind] credit themselves with a special inter-consciousness, a soul, for which they do not give other creatures credit."[8]

Land and a Theology of Place

Traditionally, our Native Americans understand all creation to have spirit, soul, or life force—what some would call panentheism. It is important to note that there is a direct correlation between the treatment of the land and the treatment of people, especially women and BIPOC (Black, Indigenous, People of Color).

7. Quoted in George Madison Bodge, *Soldiers in King Philip's War: Being a Critical Account of That War, with a Concise History of the Indian Wars of New England from 1620–1677* (Leominster, MA: n.p., 1896), 15.

8. Conrad M. Arensberg and Arthur H. Niehoff, *Introducing Social Change: A Manual for Community Development* (Chicago: Aldine, 1971), 224.

This makes it possible, as we talk about theologies of place and examples of Western abstract theologies, to espouse a view of creation care without what Indigenous theologians would call a theology of place. A local theology developed from within a local community and a local theology of place that considers the social history, the geologic factors, the seasons, and so on should be of primary importance to a creation theology, or any type of theology. In his book *The Land*, Walter Brueggemann challenges biblical theology, stating, "Land is central, if not *the* central theme of biblical faith. Land functions as a prism through which other aspects of Israel's faith can be seen."[9]

When land is lost, a history is ended. It takes land to make history. Humanity is in direct relationship with the land and all creation, a principle found throughout the scriptures and in some of the most poetic places, like Job 12:7–10, where Job says,

> Just ask the animals, and they will teach you.
>   Ask the birds of the sky, and they will tell you.
> Speak to the earth, and it will instruct you.
>   Let the fish in the sea speak to you.
> For they all know
>   that my disaster has come from the hand of the
>   LORD.
> For the life of every living thing is in his hand,
>   and the breath of every human being.

God loves everything in creation (John 3:16). In the stories we find God counting the clouds (Job 38:37), releasing the rain

---

9. Walter Brueggemann, *The Land: Place as Gift, Promise, and Challenge in Biblical Faith* (Philadelphia: Fortress, 1977), 3.

(5:10), directing the snow (37:6; 38:22), knowing when a sparrow falls (Matt. 10:29), knowing where a donkey is tied (21:2), knowing where the fish will swim (John 21:6), adorning the lilies of the field (Matt. 6:29–30), and comparing the ostrich and the stork (Job 39:13). At the time of Jesus, there were lots of modern mechanisms, lots of inventions. You had chariots and wheels and waterwheels and little torches and all kinds of mechanistic things. But we find Jesus mostly talking about the things that grow out of the earth and the things that fly above the earth and the things that are planted in the earth.

Jesus, like every Jewish person, would have included land as part of his own understanding of who God is. Narratives around place naturally compel us to define our social location in the story. A nonlocal theology, a more abstract theology, makes it easier to ignore social location and place. This Western view encourages an objective view of reality over a subjective view of reality, like the only things that matter are those we can prove, as opposed to our thoughts, our hearts, and our experiences. Which is more correct? Some consider this split to be a false dichotomy of reality. How do these views of reality relate to propositional truth? How do they relate to hermeneutics? How do they relate to expository preaching? How do they relate to narrative theology or to pedagogy?

Here is a quote from 1978 from one of our traditional people, as he talked about our harmony way in a way that our Cherokee people understood. He said:

> In the language of my people: there's a word for land, eloheh, the same word also means history, culture and religion. We cannot separate our place on earth from our lives on the earth, nor from our vision, nor our meaning as a people. We are taught from childhood that the animals and even the trees and plants

are our brothers and sisters, so we, when we speak of land, we're not speaking of the property or territory or even a piece of ground upon which our houses sit and our crops are grown. We are speaking of something truly sacred.[10]

The Harmony of Creation

So many religions, including what is often taught in various forms of Christianity, Buddhism, Hinduism, and in the theory of evolution, and so on, espouse ideas that assert or at least imply that human beings are the pinnacle of the created order, including dominion or reincarnation or the evolutionary order.

Indigenous creation narratives invariably reveal human beings as the cooperative partner with the rest of creation, participating with creation in an important role, usually as caretakers. Even those Indigenous creation narratives that lack human beings can serve to remind us that creation can exist without us. The biblical concept of shalom, salvation, or healing in many ways can be equated directly with the Native American concept of restoration or harmony. The Creator's plan for harmony concerns all of creation, the whole community of creation, not just humanity.

I think human beings are the only creatures who willfully reject their created state and therefore must make a choice to return to normalcy, which is a state of harmony. This can occur through many truth paths, but I believe each path leads to Christ and each has implications for all creation. Harmony of all creation can be understood in and through Christ, as the Creator-Restorer of shalom or harmony to the world. This is evident in the following passages:

10. Brian Edward Brown, *Religion, Law, and the Land: Native Americans and the Judicial Interpretation of Sacred Land* (Santa Barbara, CA: Greenwood, 1999), 38.

God created everything through him, / and nothing was created except through him. (John 1:3)

He came into the very world he created, but the world didn't recognize him. (1:10)

For through him God created everything / in the heavenly realms and on earth. / He made the things we can see / and the things we can't see— / such as thrones, kingdoms, rulers, and authorities in the unseen world. / Everything was created through him and for him. / He existed before anything else, / and he holds all creation together. (Col. 1:16–17)

Long ago God spoke many times and in many ways to our ancestors through the prophets. And now in these final days, he has spoken to us through his Son. God promised everything to the Son as an inheritance, and through the Son he created the universe. (Heb. 1:1–2)

But for us, / There is one God, the Father, / by whom all things were created, / and for whom we live. / And there is one Lord, Jesus Christ, / through whom all things were created, / and through whom we live. (1 Cor. 8:6)

An honest, shalom-based salvation or healing is not ethereal but very much earthbound. We should be suspicious of salvation theologies that hold a future in heaven as more important to us than our time on earth is now. Shalom, or harmony, is primarily about now. Our most famous religious leader, a leader in our Cherokee past, was a man named Redbird Smith. In 1918 he said, "Our religion does not teach me to concern myself with the life that shall be after this, but it does teach me to be concerned with what my everyday life should be."[11] This sort of

11. Cherokee oral tradition.

reminds me of when Jesus said, "Don't worry about tomorrow, for tomorrow will bring its own worries" (Matt. 6:34), and, "On earth, as it is in heaven" (6:10). Imbalance like genocide or enslavement or mass land theft, left unreconciled, ensures that no shalom in the land is possible. Hundreds of Indigenous nations have suffered a similar fate. The European genocide against Native Americans was planned and calculated like those of Hitler and Stalin. The perceived problem with Indians was because they held the land, the land others wanted—lands Christians wanted. Yet it was considered by the Natives to be the Creator's land. Tens of millions were killed and displaced for it.

The North American Myth and Its Influence

If you live in the Americas or another colonized country, you are a direct beneficiary of this genocide and theft. Consider your forebearers, and ask what effect this has or should have on your own spirituality. The North American myth problematizes "the other" and blames the victim for resistance. This myth has a central motif, or metanarrative, that universalizes that metanarrative through systems such as history, theology, economy, family, education, and religion. It subordinates anything contrary to the myth. Those who differ or resist are considered by Europeans traitors, unpatriotic, or labeled with a dangerous ideology (like critical race theory) and thereby dismissed. For example, American Indigenous people were considered to be the original terrorists on this continent.[12]

12. One example of numerous commentaries was by L. Frank Baum, author of *The Wizard of Oz*, who advocated extermination of all Indians. J. J. Sutherland, "L. Frank Baum Advocated Extermination of Native Americans," NPR, October 27, 2010, https://www.npr.org/sections/thetwo-way/2010/10/27/130862391/l-frank-baum-advocated-extermination-of-native-americans.

Indigenous people can be drunks, we can be noble savages, we can be mascots, we can be angry Indians, but we can never be fully and equally human. A White Australian, Christopher Budden, wrote a book called *Following Jesus in Invaded Space*, which I highly recommend. Budden's thesis is that without an honest beginning among Western theologians, unrighteous invasion will continue to be fitted into the European worldview and theology as normal, and racism will continue to include White privilege and White normalcy. The way forward is both structural and relational, requiring theological thought concerning the following points: Racism is still a part of societal life, and it shapes our perceptions, our discourses, and our relatedness. Second, peoples, including the church, live on stolen land. And initial relationships on the land were based on violence, a violence that still distorts those relationships.[13]

The church must determine a social location and understand how it affects its vision and the interest it continues to protect. Indigenous people continue to be marginalized in most areas of life. Truths, as non-facts, are found in many places of human origin stories. Lessons in Native American stories from the Trickster, a common demigod-type character found in many tribal traditions, can show us that we are just human beings, and all of us are in need of help from Creator in order to find truth. The kind of consistent truth leading to shalom, or harmony, is found by observing creation and by listening to our own clear hearts. All other revelation is suspect but may still contain truth. This includes all religions, sacred writings, stories, symbols, ceremonies, traditions, prophecies, and community values. But listening to the lived experiences of those who don't get to write history is paramount.

13. Christopher Budden, *Following Jesus in Invaded Space: Doing Theology on Aboriginal Land* (Eugene, OR: Pickwick, 2009).

Linda Smith, a Maori living in Aotearoa (New Zealand), wrote:

> Concern about "the indigenous problem" began as an explicitly militaristic or policing concern. . . .
>
> Once indigenous peoples had been rounded up and put on reserves the "indigenous problem" became embedded as a policy discourse which reached out across all aspects of a government's attempt to control the natives. Both "friends of the natives" and those hostile to indigenous peoples conceptualized the issues of colonization and European encroachment on indigenous territories in terms of a problem of the natives. The natives were, according to this view, to blame for not accepting the terms of their colonization. . . . The belief in the "indigenous problem" is still present in the Western psyche.[14]

The good news of healing is that Great Mystery, or truth, is Christ. All other truth, regardless of where it may be found, points to Christ. The good news is therefore an early introduction to Christ, which gives us the power to live a life of integrity in truthful shalom or harmony, to seek community and influence the greater community toward truth, to create a sense of shalom or harmony, and to live out salvation or healing, here on earth and in harmony with the whole community of creation.

Constructing New Models

To understand why the earth seems in chaos, we must perceive the theological dualism found in Western Enlightenment and that whole worldview where human beings can be categorized

---

14. Linda Tuhiwai Smith, "Problematizing the Indigenous Is a Western Obsession," in *Decolonizing Methodologies: Research and Indigenous Peoples*, 2nd ed. (London: Zed Books, 2012), 94–95.

apart from creation. The result is the false dichotomy between
the physical earth and spiritual beings. In a harmony-based
worldview, human beings are fully physical and the earth is
fully spiritual. Therefore healing, or salvation if you will, by
definition should always consider the healing of people, healing
of our history of colonialism and neo-colonialism, and healing
of all of the community of creation. All of creation is sacred,
and there is a problem with one's worldview when one is considered sacred and not the other. Jesus's worldview displays this
when he says, "But I say, do not make any vows! Do not say, 'By
heaven!' because heaven is God's throne. And do not say, 'By
the earth!' because the earth is his footstool" (Matt. 5:34–35).
Jesus understands everything to be God's sacred creation. In
the hegemony of Western bias, human beings are categorized
apart from, and over, creation, resulting in a false sense of superiority and a dichotomy between a physical earth and us as
spiritual beings. But there are other stories where humans are
fully physical and fully spiritual and creation is fully spiritual
and fully physical. Mother Earth is alive!

Along with a worldview of foundational dualism naturally
comes the hierarchy of humans over creation and the hierarchy
of humans over other human beings via gender, race, class, and
such. Emerson and Smith state:

> Two factors are most striking about evangelical solutions to
> racial problems. First, they are profoundly individualistic and
> interpersonal: become a Christian, love your individual neigh-
> bors, establish a cross-race friendship, give individuals the right
> to pursue jobs and individual justice without discrimination by
> other individuals, and ask forgiveness of individuals one has
> wronged. Second, although several evangelicals discuss the per-
> sonal sacrifice necessary to form friendships across race, their

solutions do not require financial or cultural sacrifice. They do not advocate or support changes that might cause extensive discomfort or change their economic and cultural lives. In short, they maintain what is for them the noncostly status quo.[15]

New models need constructing. Ignorance needs correcting. Comfort needs sacrificing. Reparations need to be normalized. Charles Eastman Ohiyesa, a Dakota medical doctor, said, "Long before I ever heard of Christ or saw a white man, I had learned from an untutored woman the essence of morality. With the help of dear Nature herself, she taught me things simple but of mighty import. I knew God. I perceived what goodness is. I saw and loved what is really beautiful. Civilization has not taught me anything better!"[16]

My Kiowa mother said it this way: "Before the White man came, we knew who God was. We knew God was the Creator. We knew God was powerful. We knew God was loving. We knew God was sacred. We didn't quite know how much God loved us, because we didn't know the story of Jesus." Then she looked at me and said, "But we were this close" (holding her fingers apart an inch). "But when the missionaries came and gave us their theology, that made the gap as wide as the Grand Canyon."

15. Michael O. Emerson and Christian Smith, *Divided by Faith: Evangelical Religion and the Problem of Race in America* (New York: Oxford University Press, 2000), 38.

16. Charles A. Eastman Ohiyesa, *The Soul of the Indian* (1911; repr., n.p.: Digital Scanning, Inc., 2001), 29.

Question and Response

I have always wondered about the term *Mother Earth*. Could you speak to the meaning of this?

Women are sacred because they can bring forth children. The earth brings forth everything, as even Paul says in Romans 8:22, "The whole creation has been groaning in labor pains until now" (NRSV). I think this is a pretty basic understanding of what the earth is all about, which is giving birth to new life, thus, Mother Earth.

How do I develop community in a city and develop a theology of the land in a metropolitan area?

That's a really good question. There's a good alliance that can be made through urban permaculture folks who are actually trying to create food systems in urban areas and involving oneself with urban gardens. Cooperatives, CSAs, even something just as simple as growing a tomato plant on your deck. If you only have a four-by-six deck, you can still grow a tomato plant, and you can learn a whole lot from a tomato plant. So I think there are ways to do that, but you need to get your hands dirty.

It's a shame that our cities are not built differently. They could be constructed differently. There are cities like Curitiba, Brazil, that have done some great things in experimenting with creating a city that is more holistic and friendly and nature-oriented than our American cities are. Urban areas don't have to be full of concrete and glass and brick and mortar. They can also be built to include parks and plazas and gardens. When I speak to groups of young people, I always challenge them by telling them, "You know what to do! You have a calling to be an urban ranger or a forest service person, or is your calling to be a city planner or to be a mayor of a city, or a city council person?" Those are the people who influence our cities and those are the people who need to be thinking theologically when it comes to how to rebuild our cities. And as buildings come down in urban areas all over, that's the time to begin to reconstruct in a way that makes more sense for the future and more sense theologically and ecologically.

For somebody who feels disconnected from the land, what are some ways to listen to and to observe creation? What are some ways to be open to being taught if you haven't had the experience of asking the animals and allowing them to teach you?

Perhaps just going out with that same question and spending time in creation is the way you get taught. You asked the question, "How do I learn while being out there?" In one of my classes called Theology and Ethic of the Land, I ask people to go out for two hours on the land, and they can take a journal with them to take a few notes, but I don't want them writing a lot, mostly just observing creation around them. Then we come back and we share. Initially, when I first did that, I thought we might just get a couple words here and there, but in actuality, the sharing usually lasts for two hours. They've gone out, spent time doing what is very natural, and they're open to learn from creation. I think you just have to be open and decide that you're going to learn from creation while you are out there. There's a point where you have to stop thinking about all the things that are bothering you and actually watch what's going on around you. I find that those are the times when Creator speaks to me the most, and usually the deepest. I don't think there's any special trick to it. I think anybody can do it. You just have to be willing to be taught.

It sounds like you're positing that an Indigenous Christian theology might be panentheistic. How would you comment on that in relation to the traditional Western Christian view of monotheism?

Well, I'm not sure that those categories are really helpful in this case, because we're pitting one against the other, when I think they can actually be the same. Panentheism simply recognizes that everything that is created is alive and has some sort of animation, or being, soul, or spirit. However it might be put, there's something else going on there. I think that the converse question is probably even more important. Explain to me how it's not alive, because you can't do it from a quantum physics perspective. I think plastic may be the only thing that doesn't have spirit; I'm not sure. But take metal for instance. It's just sitting there, but on a subatomic level, it's moving; it's not stationary, because it's from the earth. It's not just an object, but it's an object that's interacting with other materials around it. There are probably ways to come around to that scientifically, but it just doesn't make sense to me at least to think that there's not some sort of life in everything that God has created. So I guess I would throw the question back at you: How do you figure that it's not alive?

I'm interested in the contrasts you listed between Western theology and Indigenous theology. Can you list anything that is not a contrast, but actually a complement?

If you are looking at it from a Christian perspective, perhaps there's a lot of commonality between our understandings of

Spirit, or the Holy Spirit. But when the comparison becomes a positional, versus a relational, trinitarian view, then I think there is trouble reconciling the two. And, of course, there are lots of folks coming around to a social trinitarian view lately. There are new things happening all the time in theology. When I talk about Western worldview and Indigenous worldview, I don't by any means want to say that this is what all Indigenous people believe, and this is what all Westerners believe. But these are majority views that we have to deal with that have taken up most of our histories, so there is a lot of commonality.

There's a lot of complementing. I think one of the ways that Western folks complement and help Indigenous theology is through superficial categorization: the ability to continually break apart categories and create new categories and make discoveries within those categories. We're getting wonderful medical discoveries because of this type of Western categorization and careful examination. The problem is that if we try to live out of those reduced categories, we're not living out of a whole reality; we're living out of partial reality. So the problem is bringing it back to the whole.

I have peripheral neuropathy in my feet from my diabetes, and so I have a podiatrist and I have a neurologist to treat this ailment. I also have a cardiologist because I have atrial fibrillation. Those are particular categories that people excelled in and examined as part of the whole human body, and by disease as well, and there are little things that they discovered as a result. Those particular sciences were perfected as a result. But if they don't talk to one another and treat me like a whole being, then I'm probably in a lot of trouble. What happens if one begins to operate without consulting the others? If they think their area is more important than the whole of the reality of my being and my body, then I might be in trouble.

I wonder about original sin in the context of Jesus being a redeemer. Do Indigenous people have a sense of rebellion against God, who is spirit and not material?

I actually think that was something that came about largely under Augustine and Jerome and Ambrose, and some other folks who were basically giving total control of people's salvation to the Catholic Church at the time. I don't think the Bible teaches that, so therefore, I don't believe it. But I do believe that we are all humans who make mistakes, and hopefully, we learn from our mistakes. On to redemption. So, what is Christ's role to restore harmony? The disruption of harmony is by not accepting our own limitedness, both individually and corporately and structurally. Christ came to save us or, better said, to heal us, so that we can be people who restore harmony. That's my understanding, and this healing is not just individual but is about healing together. God is interested in the whole community of creation, not just human souls but everything.

Are you hopeful that Western culture will ever change?

If I wasn't, I don't think I'd be here or I'd be speaking out at all. But I can tell you that there have been plenty of times when I wanted to just retreat out of Western civilization altogether. For years I fought that inclination to just dial out, but I realized that is not Christ's intention for me or for our world. We've all got to get there together. Regardless of how difficult it may look, we move ahead together. Somebody once told me that sometimes you come up against a brick wall and you have to bang your head against the brick wall and you know that the wall is not going to move and you know your head is going to bleed—but it's the right thing to do, so you do it anyway. I think that's probably more descriptive of how I feel than anything, but there's still some hope.

You referred to the Trickster. What is the Trickster?

Trickster is the one in our stories who comes and is often sort of the wayward being who is always trying to trick you into something silly or bad. The Trickster is in many of our Indigenous stories and in some tribal traditions is a coyote. In my tribe, Trickster is Jis-du, or Rabbit. He comes and he tries to show you a lesson of how to live, and Trickster then ends up getting tricked himself somehow through it all. We learn our lessons of how not to live through Trickster stories.

One question I sometimes get asked is, So what do we do with the brutality of nature? How did a good Creator make such brutal things? And, if we can somehow see this as just part of the harmony, does that allow brutality to be condoned as natural and good? I think you learn different things from different creatures. The problem of evil is one of those that we're all still working on. But the idea is that if nature is in harmony, doesn't that mean everything should be harmonious as if it were a utopian-type world? No. It just means that everything is doing what it was created to do. I said this earlier: Indigenous theology is an oxymoron because the most ideal logic, the most profound theological thought I have is the name for Creator, the Great Mystery. We are very limited in our understanding. We don't understand everything about creation; we don't understand much about Creator; and then add to that, we're trying to understand ourselves. But I think we have enough understanding to know how to live.

How far back do we go with reparations? Do we go to the Gaelic Wars or to the Chinese dynasties?

Perhaps, if you're living in China you do. But if we're living in America, and I can only speak for the United States because that's the history I know, then we have to deal with what has occurred on our own land.

Sometimes there can be the assumption that these unjust things have ended. On the contrary, these things are still going on, both from the sort of ripple effect they have in the lives of descendants, the ramifications of what happened and post-traumatic stress and the re-traumatization, and from the injustices that continue to be done daily. You know it wasn't that long ago you may have heard about the Dakota Access Pipeline at Standing Rock. Our elders and spiritual leaders had their eagle-feather headdresses ripped off their heads and thrown on the ground. They were then thrown in dog cages and given numbers on their arms like the Nazis did in the concentration camps during the Jewish Holocaust.

So these things are still continuing because the worldviews are still the same among settlers, and that worldview props up the presumed superiority. The assumed right of White folks over Native folks is still present among police, in armies, in government, and so on, so it's not necessarily a problem just of the past. That's why I think we have to deal with it. You can replace everybody in a dysfunctional system with people who have the opposite idea of the old system, and yet that system may still be an evil system. The systemic structure has to be dealt with, and often when we're dealing with systems, there are people who want to improve the system, and there are people who were not part of making that system who want to be a part of making a new system. Sometimes we speak over each other.

What do reparations look like to you?

I think that has to be decided in every community and in every locale. I think the lead role is that of the community receiving the reparations. The junior partner is that of the settler folk, and they work on that together and figure out what that means in their context. That might mean remuneration of money in some places. It might mean land in others; it might mean both or other creative things. I think we need a lot of creative thinking. I think that when we just talk about money as reparations, it's very shortsighted. I'm not against money, but I don't think that is going to really help the relationship going forward. So in my last lecture I discussed awareness, lamenting together, reparations, and creative thinking concerning reparations, and then memorializing that so future generations know. So I think there are ways to do that, but I don't think there's any one prescription.

Do we need to abandon the stories we grew up with as we learn from other stories, or how can we keep true to our story while doing that dance together?

Along the lines of personal discipleship, for some people it might mean complete abandonment of one story or the other, but for others, it might mean synthesizing the stories. You know, I can't speak to someone else's spirituality. I wouldn't try to tell anybody what to do. I can only tell you what I have done, in trying to live with the spirituality that I've been taught and in trying to live within both worldviews. For me, sometimes those are integrative. Sometimes I'm throwing things out, and sometimes I've probably thrown the baby out with the bathwater, but that's the life that I have to live and figure out as I go. This walk with Creator is uncontrollable. When we try to control it, that's one indicator that it's a pretty sure thing we are doing something wrong. What I hear you say is, "I'm coming out from American colonization-dominating culture, so I want to control it." So, I'm saying, don't. Go with the flow and see where it takes you.

We all have our common humanity and one thing that cuts across all lines is poverty. Can you comment on that?

Poverty is one of those common bridges that we can use that cuts across our humanity. Everybody has some sort of privilege somewhere in their life, and therefore, we all can be considered somewhat of an oppressor. Our particular privilege, or lack thereof, doesn't take away from the whole dynamic that I've been talking about, but what it says is that poverty doesn't discriminate. Certainly, abuse of the female gender cuts across all ethnicity and race as well. So, there's a lot of common, human things that we must work through together, and that reminds us in some sense that we're not so different from one another.

Can you speak to the difference between communal thinking and individualistic thinking: How is the Indigenous way of knowing different, and how does that relate to our understandings of salvation and personal sin?

So, you've heard the phrase *Indigenous way*? "I am, because we are." In the Western world it's "We are, because I am." That may seem like a subtle difference, but actually it is paramount. First and foremost, by way of design, I think all human beings are made for community. I believe when Jesus formed the called-out ones, the *ekklēsia*, it was about forming alternative communities, not about calling out a bunch of individuals. As I look in the New Testament at the spread of the early church, the Ethiopian eunuch was the only person not associated with a community of faith and, of course, tradition says that he founded the Coptic church in Ethiopia.

The church in North America has come through all of our individualized Greco-Roman influence, and especially through the Enlightenment. We've become so highly individualized that we really can't read the scriptures accurately. It's very difficult for us to read the scriptures from anything but a Western, American, middle-class perspective, because it's all about me. But it's not all about me; it's about we! I don't think that anyone wrote the scriptures for me. I think the scriptures were written for me as I live in and with my community.

If someone comes to the Genesis creation story with a colonial mentality, as opposed to a caretaker perspective, they miss part of the story. Are there other parts that we need to see in a fresh way that our preconceptions are hindering us from seeing?

Yes. I think scripture is story, and every story has what Ricoeur calls "surplus of meaning."[17] I'll give you an example from my life. I'm in seminary doing my Master of Divinity education, and in my freshman year one of my professors says, "You need to see through your Indigenous eyes." I'm like, "What does that mean?" I think I mentioned this was a struggle with me for a long time. After struggling for years, I started reading some passages differently. No longer was it "I'm just going to go and read some of my familiar passages." I had to ask, "What's going on in the story?"

For example, I looked at Luke 15. Luke 15 is a story. Luke 15:1–2 says that the Pharisees and scribes began to grumble

---

17. *Stanford Encyclopedia of Philosophy*, s.v. "Paul Ricoeur," accessed June 15, 2021, https://plato.stanford.edu/entries/ricoeur/.

and complain because Jesus received sinners and even ate with them. That's the context for the story. Then Jesus tells three stories: one about lost sheep, one about a lost coin, and one about lost sons. So, I started thinking more about how my elders would see this story. All of a sudden I realized, there's something there that I never saw before because I was trained to think that this story is all about evangelism. You know, you go out and you bring that lost sheep in and you find that lost coin, and in the lost son section, he is found and that's all what the story is about.

So I was overlooking this part: in each section it mentions the whole community. Each time they come back to a community, and the community celebrates with them. After that, I really began to understand more of what shalom is about. In our Indigenous harmony way, and some of my dissertation is about the values that I discovered in this process, I began to look at that scripture and say, "What was Jesus trying to teach these Pharisees?" They are people who know the scriptures, but now I've seen something different. So, what are the three stories wrapped within one big story about?

Well, first of all I realized that they are not three separate stories—they're one story. Second, I'm looking to understand shalom in Jesus's own context, harmony way in my own, using as the litmus test: Are you taking care of the widows? Are you taking care of the orphans? Are you taking care of the immigrants? And then I began to understand. That first story is about a gentile shepherd, as many were at the time. The second story is about a widow. The third story is about an orphan son, who actually made himself an orphan. I'm pretty sure that what Jesus was saying when he told them those three stories, which are really just one story, was basically, "You are not fulfilling the harmony way; you are not living out shalom." The kingdom that Jesus preached was the Shalom Kingdom. Those are the kinds of things that I began to look at, and I realized I've really missed so much. I have to continually train myself to look at scripture through my Indigenous eyes.

For two years I didn't read the Bible. Instead I heard it, like story. I decided that if I needed to read something from scripture, I'd have my wife or someone else read it to me. I just wanted to hear the story orally, and you know, that taught me more than probably any other time of learning. I look at scripture to understand the story and what's going on in the story. And when I understand the story, I think, maybe I'm seeing it through Indigenous eyes. And that's one of the things that I think the West needs help with.

What is the Indigenous understanding of the reason why the Creator created in the first place?

I cannot answer that question because there is no single answer. There are thousands of Indigenous nations all across America, and each might have a different way of explaining that, and in my traditions, I could not speak for all. But I can tell you my understanding. The stories lead us back to being people who maintain and restore harmony. Another thing that is occurring in our Cherokee stories is that the hero is the one you would least expect. Usually, the smallest creature comes and saves the day. We were made to do great things. We're made to keep the balance; we're made to keep the harmony.

I understand the Trinity as a Community of Creator. I don't just talk about Trinity because the creeds say *Trinity*. I think about starting with creation and asking, What are God's fingerprints on all of creation? Remember how I talked about how there is nothing singular, even down to the smallest quarks within the atom? And so, there's this infinite unity and diversity that works in all of creation, so that must reflect Creator. So I'm starting on the earth and I'm going back and understanding shalom as Jesus's mission. And so then, for me, the Trinity—if we want to use the terms *Father, Son, Holy Spirit*, that's fine— are perfect shalom and live in perfect harmony, preferring and deferring to one another.

The Community of Creator decides we're going to make human beings and all of creation along with that, and invite all of that world into shalom living, and so Jesus comes to earth as a human being. But not simply as a human being but as a marginalized human being. He hangs out with the disenfranchised of society, teaches about taking care of the most marginalized among us. All those things show us that this is how you know you have shalom—how are the least of these doing? Then he invites us to be communities of shalom, reflecting the very Community of Creator, the Trinity. And so for me, that's the purpose. We are here because God exists in shalom, and God desires that we create shalom on earth.

Well, just one more thing about Trinity. I always think to myself, *What does it take to be community?* Well, if God is one by God-self, then that's not diversity. That's sort of like, you know, maybe the royal monarchy. I don't know much about monarchy, but as one, God is a benevolent dictator. Or God as two becomes a partnership of two benevolent dictators. But the first possibility for community is three. So now you have A, B, and C, and there are a lot of permutations that are only possible in three. I don't have trouble going along with the Trinity idea because it takes Trinity to create community, and community is the basis of shalom.

You mentioned universal salvation, and how truth is in all things, and I was wondering which side do you stand on

concerning the road to heaven or hell? Not all roads lead to heaven, do they?

So, I don't think those are the only two options. I think that what I can say about my understanding is that all truth points to Jesus and all truth is a reflection of Jesus. This is my own belief. If I find truth in any other system, or anywhere else, that truth is pointing to Jesus.

So, do you think that someone in that other system could arrive at "salvation"?

Do I think that they could meet Christ and not know Christ's name? Yes, I do.

3

Decolonizing Western Christian Theology

At one point in my life I was what was called a "commissioned missionary." I spent two years in Kodiak, Alaska, working with Inuit, Aleut, and other troubled teens as a teaching-parent at the Kodiak Baptist Mission. I call those my "missionary oppressor" years. This time was a great conflict in terms of trying to set them on the right path with the behavioral modification model that violated their cultural standards, and it about drove me crazy. After two years I decided I needed further education, and my pastor suggested I go to seminary. My response was, "Seminary? I know I've heard that word before, but what does 'seminary' mean again?" Eventually, I did go to seminary to study for an MDiv.

While I was in seminary, I discovered the life of another person quite obscure and mostly forgotten to history. I was hoping to write a book about this missionary, whose letters and journals I got to know by reading through the twelve boxes of them that were archived. He was a missionary among my people, the Cherokee, and his name was Evan Jones. Jones was a Welshman who came to America in the early part of the nineteenth century. As far as missionaries go, he did a pretty good job. Basically, my question during my time in seminary was, "How do I serve among my own Indigenous people without oppressing them?" That was really why I went to seminary. Through reading all twelve boxes of Jones's original journals and letters, I discovered some principles for my own ministry. After seminary I was commissioned as a missionary among Indigenous people in Oklahoma.

I was hoping to eventually write a book about Jones, and when I did my PhD, I thought my dissertation might be on Jones. But at the time I felt that a better service could be rendered for our Indigenous communities by writing about something else. That "something else" is the first part of this essay. The title of my PhD dissertation was "The Harmony Way: Integrating Indigenous Values within Native North American Theology and Mission."[1]

The Harmony Way

I asked a couple questions in my dissertation: Do our various Native American peoples have a generally shared set of values that could guide the construction of new models for mission and theology in North American Native communities? And if so, to what degree are these values shared among Native American communities? In addition, what resources, particularly values, are available within Native American communities

1. Randy S. Woodley, "The Harmony Way: Integrating Indigenous Values within Native North American Theology and Mission" (PhD diss., Asbury Theological Seminary, 2010).

themselves for developing appropriate models of mission and theology, and could such resources be developed into authentic integral models? So those were the questions that I began with. I also had a biblical/theological construction of shalom based on Walter Brueggemann's work, a contextually informed anthropology in missiology, and an Indigenous construction of decolonization and indigenization for mission and theology. I used literature from other fields such as anthropology education, psychology, history, sociology, and religion.

I had extensive interviews with eight elders who spoke their languages and who were spiritual leaders in their communities, and I surveyed a hundred Native Americans from almost every region of the United States and Canada. Those responses were analyzed using grounded theory as a way to discover and organize the system of values. The surveys, the elder interviews, and the responses with literature regarding Native American value studies were all linked. As the values categories emerged, I was able to establish among Native Americans a widely held construct referred to generally as "the harmony way." Now, I had already had some suspicion that this harmony-way construct was present, as I knew it was in my own people. I also knew it was identifiable among the Navajo, but I wanted to see how widespread it was among our Indigenous peoples in North America. I was then able to deduce, isolate, and examine ten core values that exist within the framework of the Native American harmony way. These are commonly held among all forty-five tribal groups represented in the study.

For each elder that I interviewed, every single interview went just like this: I would say, "Among my people we have a construct called *eloheh*. It means everything is in harmony. Everything is in balance. The ground is producing what it should, nobody's at war, and people are generally happy." About that time they would break in and say something like, "Oh yes, we have that also, and it is called . . ." Each language had its own word to describe the harmony way. Then I allowed them to talk about that for as long as they liked. I merged all that information together, and I came up with ten harmony-way values. I cannot say that they are "universal values" among all Indigenous peoples, because my findings only represent forty-five tribal groups. But they represent nearly every region of North America, so I can say that there is a widespread construct of the harmony way. Here are the values that I found to constitute the harmony way.

1. Tangible spirituality/our spirituality must be practiced
   - belief in the Great Mystery/Creator
   - all creation is both natural and spiritual
   - continued involvement in ceremonies and traditions
   - support of tribal societies; they are vital
   - use of symbols in everyday life
   - authority comes from reflected experience, not from information

   Summation: The earth and everything on it is sacred. *"Respect everyone. Everything is sacred."*

2. Our lives are governed by harmony
   - seek to maintain balance in all of life
   - life in harmony is expressed as a circle or a hoop
   - seek peace
   - humans are mostly good with some evil
   - fear is a catalyst for virtue

   Summation: Everything on earth is at its best when seeking peace, harmony, and balance. *"Seek harmony."*

3. Community is essential
   - women are sacred
   - children are loved
   - elders are respected
   - family is vital
   - everyone is integrally related

   Summation: We are remarkably related to everyone and everything, so accept your huge family. *"Increase your friends and family."*

4. Humor is sacred and necessary
   - humor is part of the balance
   - both impromptu and designed in ceremony

   Summation: Humor reminds us we are just human beings. *"Laugh at yourself."*

5. Feeling of cooperation/communality
   - consensus gives dignity
   - high tolerance—dissension is respected
   - process includes both hearts and minds
   - diversity gives strength and balance to life

   Summation: *"Everyone gets a say."*

6. Oral communication and traditions
   - words have primordial power and should be used cautiously
   - traditions are passed on orally
   - stories are the main vehicle for teaching and sustaining
   - quiet, respectful communication

   Summation: *"Speak from your heart."*

7. Present and past time orientation
- present engagement overrides future scheduling ("Indian time")
- fluidity between past and present
- future is determined by looking to the past

Summation: *"Look forward by looking back."*

8. Open work ethic
- meaningful work
- work only as needed
- identity is in both doing and being
- lifestyle with few constraints

Summation: *"Work hard but rest well."*

9. Great hospitality/generosity
- shown through giving gifts in ceremony
- open home ethic, sharing resources, food, etc.

Summation: *"Share what you have."*

10. Natural connectedness to all creation
- reciprocity
- co-sustainer, steward (keeper)
- gratitude expressed in ceremony
- learning with creation—a dynamic, organic process

Summation: *"We are all related."*

Forty-five tribal groups share these values. At Asbury Seminary, we had about 60 percent of the folks from other countries represented. I had already spent a lot of time with different Indigenous peoples from around the world, and I came to find out as I was doing this data collection, and as we would talk to one another, that the Indigenous students from all around the world also had a similar construct—from the Aboriginals in the lands now called Australia, to the Maori in Aotearoa (New Zealand), the Zulu in South Africa, the Maasai in Samburu and in Kenya, the Ikallahan on the northern island of the Philippines, and the Hawaiians on their islands (aloha!). I was able to sit down with Walter Brueggemann once, and I asked him, "You know, I had this experience when I was doing all this, and I wondered if I would be overstating it if I said these values and this harmony way sound very much like humanity's original instructions?" And he said, "Absolutely not, you would not be overstating your case." Brueggemann found the same thing all over the world as well.

Harmony and Shalom

We are all Indigenous from somewhere even if it is hidden deep in our DNA. I strongly encourage people to find their own indigeneity in whatever form they would like to do that. So, our Indigenous harmony-way constructs are much like the ancient Jewish concept of shalom. The shalom word group often translates as peace, restoration of creation, prosperity, respect, justice, truth, acceptance, restitution, abundance, equity, integrity, intimacy, growth, well-being, restored relationship, and a place where God is in charge. It is a word pregnant with meaning. To quote Brueggemann, "Shalom is the end of coercion. Shalom is the end of fragmentation. Shalom is the freedom to rejoice. Shalom is the courage to live an integrated life in a community of coherence. These are not simply neat values to be added on, but they are massive protests against the central values by which our world operates. The world depends on coercion. The world depends on fragmented loyalties. The world as presently ordered depends on these very conditions, against which the gospel protects and to which it provides alternatives."[2]

And here's a good picture in the New Testament of what shalom looks like: "Most important of all, continue to show deep love for each other, for love covers a multitude of sins. Cheerfully share your home with those who need a meal or a place to stay. God has given each of you a gift from his great variety of spiritual gifts. Use them well to serve one another. Do you have the gift of speaking? Then speak as though God himself were speaking through you. Do you have the gift of helping others? Do it with all the strength and energy that God supplies" (1 Pet. 4:8–11). I think for the New Testament writers and for Jesus himself, these values were embedded in their thinking. How else do we conceive of shalom?

We see God's intended shalom throughout the biblical festivals (Num. 28–29), the Genesis creation passages (Gen. 1–2), the Sabbath years (Lev. 25:2–7), and how a people keeps their lands. As you know, one-seventh of all land was set aside, remaining fallow each year (Exod. 23:11), and then eventually on the seventh year everything is set aside. And why is that? It's for the poor (Deut. 24:20–21), it's for the animals, for the wild animals, for the ox and other animals (25:4), and then, of course, part of that whole system has the same purpose. When you forget a bunch of grapes out in the field, leave them because other people will get them. You left a bunch of wheat out in the field. Leave it because the poor will need it to make bread. You don't glean the edges of your field because then those who need it can come and gather it.

This whole shalom-sabbath-jubilee continuum is about making sure that the most marginalized in society get taken care

2. Walter Brueggemann, *Peace: Living toward a Vision* (St. Louis: Chalice, 2001), 51.

of, including wild animals, and allowing the land to rest—everything—the whole community of creation! And you understand how pleased God is with you by how you treat the foreigners and the immigrants. You judge the measure of God's shalom by how the widows and the orphans are treated (Deut. 10:18; 27:19; Isa. 1:17; Jer. 22:3; Zech. 7:10; James 1:27). As I've looked at the scriptures with my harmony-way lenses while not interjecting too much eisegesis, I believe this is exactly what Jesus was teaching. His kingdom was a shalom kingdom. New Testament ethics, our shalom ethics, has always been tested on the margins: on the powerless, the poor, the oppressed, the disenfranchised, and the marginalized (Matt. 23:4; Mark 10:21; Luke 14:13).

The Old Testament narrative of Genesis 1–11 is a story of shalom established and then broken at every level. All the relationships affected here. Between man and woman. Between humanity and God. Between humanity and animals (skins to cover themselves in Gen. 3:21). Between humanity and the earth (expelled from the garden in 3:23). Between members of the same family ("Am I my brother's guardian?" in 4:9). Between ethnic groups with the whole story of Babel (11:1–9). Jesus's kingdom is a story of shalom. His kingdom is a place where shalom reigns. It is both old and new.

The Western Worldview and the Breaking of Shalom

Now, the story of America's Indigenous peoples is a story of shalom being established over centuries of harmony-way understanding but broken severely by the Europeans.

The Doctrine of Discovery, *Terra Nullius*, Puritan theology, Manifest Destiny, residential boarding schools, the reservation system, assimilation policies, and lawsuits like *Cobell v. Salazar* in the United States—all of these show the intentional effort of the colonizer state to break shalom with Indigenous peoples. The problem of a Western worldview displays itself: the way of life demonstrated by Western peoples leads to alienation from the earth, hostility toward others, and estrangement from all of creation. It creates a false bubble, called Western civilization, which the West feels will protect them from calamity. This false hope is built on age-old philosophical ideas handed down from Greece, Rome, England, and other Western nation-states.

I ask a serious question: What can turn the same people who call themselves by Christ's name into a people who will kill, steal, and destroy people, land, and nature with genocidal passion? Comparing the characteristics of a Western worldview, particularly that of the United States, with the characteristics of an American Indigenous worldview, is astonishing. The Western worldview is physically dualistic, morally dualistic, essentially spiritual, religiously intolerant, individualistic, extrinsically categorical, hierarchical, competitive, greed based, utopian, White supremacist, anthropocentric, triumphalist, and patriarchal. In the Western worldview, humor is reserved for the nonspiritual, words are not binding, and people must work in order just to work.

The characteristics of an American Indigenous worldview are much different: physically and morally holistic, a very tangible spirituality, egalitarian, peace seeking, cooperative, purposeful and meaningful work, a natural interconnectedness to all creation, hospitality, and generosity. In the American Indigenous worldview, life is governed by harmony, tolerance in community is essential, humor is sacred and necessary, consensus gives dignity, diversity gives strength, and words have primordial power and are not used lightly. Again, there are some wonderful aspects to a Western worldview, but those are not the ones I'm talking about here. And there are some undesirable aspects to an Indigenous worldview, but I believe I'm comparing apples to apples here. The foundation of the Western worldview fallacy is dualism.

To carry forth a Platonic Western worldview is to invest in the ethereal or spiritual or metaphysical or abstract realm to a higher degree than the physical. In the West, our thoughts and our theologies become too easily disembodied through silly notions such as the separation of the secular and the sacred, and believing God is at work in the church more than in the world. The physical sphere, such as land or good works or our bodies, all become suspect, leading to false hierarchies and binary thinking. In the Western worldview things are either right or wrong, legal or illegal, heaven or hell, sin or holiness, success or failure, civilized or primitive, introvert or extrovert, saved or lost, clean or dirty, weeds or plants, animals or varmints, and so on. This type of thinking makes it difficult for Western thinkers to hold two seemingly incompatible things in tension without having to find a resolution. This problem creates the false assumption that all things may be understood, and that every problem may be solved. It also creates superficial compartmentalization and reductionism, dividing and erroneously classifying life into many unrelated parts with little attention given to the whole.

Extrinsic categories are partial realities, and partial realities often become false realities, forgetting about the whole in important holistic concerns, especially in things like climate change, medicine, and systematic theology. Through extrinsic categorization, salvation can be applied only to our "souls" and does not address the whole earth that Jesus made. This thinking stems from dualism. Dualism almost inevitably needs to have a hierarchy, with everything being ranked greater or lesser. In the United States, equality is wrong, or at least not a preferred system. People believe this even when they call it a democracy. The results of historical Western structured systems have unfortunately created dehumanization by class, race, ethnicity, gender, religion, nationality, and so on. In the West we are not all quite human in the way I think God made us all to be human. But in our Indigenous understanding, we are humans who are a part of a much greater community of creation.

The Western notion of anthropocentrism, deeply held as a tenet of Christianity, understands humans as being above nature not simply as part of nature. The absence of hierarchy can more easily create equality and equity, but the absence of leadership does not mean anarchy. Ignatius of Antioch was likely the first to create a Christian hierarchical contextualization in about 100 CE.[3] Ignatius was trying to make it a little easier on the church suffering persecution by modeling their system off of the Roman military hierarchy. An unintended consequence happened when Christian hierarchy met the Constantinian Empire: Christendom was the result—utopianism! Utopianism is a shared myth

3. Edward Schillebeeckx, in his book *The Church with a Human Face* (New York: Crossroad, 1985), points out that the original Jesus movement was egalitarian and most likely similar in form to a loose congregationalism governed (at least by 100 CE or so) by egalitarian groups but never without leadership—originally apostolic, and later connected by evangelists and prophets—and always organized at some level. Schillebeeckx points out that by 100 CE–120 CE, Ignatius of Antioch had contextualized church structure around the military organization of imperial Rome's occupied lands that organized administration around diocese and parishes—with the bishop equaling the field general. But in Alexandria, up until the early third century, the church was ruled by co-equal boards (a council of elders as well as a council of youngers) in a generally democratic format—so there were actually at least two completely different forms of organization. It was under Cyprian (late 300s) that the church took its more-or-less Western form that has been accepted as the norm in Western Christianity. Like so many other forms of contextualization, it was their idea of contextualization in their own context, but they normalized and universalized their context to fit the whole world. Also notice that what later became titles holding demonstrable authority like *episcopoi* and *presbyteroi* were likely better understood as functional titles in the early church.

among movements that are living for another world, either in the future or in the past. It's our humanity, our human frailty, that causes us to seek perfection. Utopianism believes it is always better for us in the other world. While utopianism sounds harmless, living for the other world too often justifies unscrupulous means in this world in order to get to that desired utopian end. The ends justify the means. We need not look outside the church to find examples replete with this fallacy and the harm it has caused groups of people as well as individuals.

Individualism is another excessive Western fallacy that has been adopted by the church theologically and hermeneutically. In one of the most individualistic societies to ever live, we have come to believe that salvation is centered on the individual, that the scriptures were written for me, personally. This fallacy results in a loss of corporateness intended by the writers of scripture, and it diminishes the community that interprets the scriptures with me. The Western hermeneutic locks out all God's other creatures in creation when compared with me. But the scriptures were not written from, or for, an individualistic worldview of competitiveness over cooperation and majority rule over true consensus. In the United States we have majority rule: 51 percent wins the day, and so you are left with 49 percent who have lost, which is a surefire way to create lasting division.

And then there is White supremacy, a system believing that White, or light-skinned, people of Western European descent have the inherent right to control all governance, all knowledge, all wealth, and all power in any given system. A symptom of what I call "other-ism." It's not new. The Greeks had "barbarians." The Romans had "savages." The English had the "heathen." North Americans have Native Americans, African Americans, LGBTQ people, immigrants, Muslims, and so on. We have them all in the United States, a place that creates intolerance for difference, where laws and other systems are formed to maintain control of the cultural other or the racial other or the religious other. Modern expressions of White supremacy are White normalcy and White privilege.

In a capitalist society we must include materialism as one of the fallacies of the Western worldview. This is simply things over people—a system predicated on greed. A reporter once asked John D. Rockefeller, How much money is enough money? He replied, "Just a little bit more." Jesus saw this in his day and considered it the root of all kinds of evil (Matt. 19:22–24; cf. 1 Tim. 6:10; Heb. 13:5). We participate in a global economic system now built on those evils.

Propositional thinking is another symptom in the Western worldview and is related to dualism. Linear thinking *appears* to be more efficient than story; it is not. In the West, the story is added for entertainment, to lighten the mood or to illustrate a propositional point. I sometimes talk about the four "books" of epistemological living: creation, community/culture, our hearts, and the scriptures. These are the four books that we should study. The scriptures are in large part oral story or narrative. Large swaths of the scriptures are story, written by people of story, for people of story. Yet we have these narratives and parables reduced to numbered verses and propositional order. Does the West even understand how to interpret story? Kenneth Bailey states, "If theology is expressed in concepts and structured by philosophy and logic, then the primary tools required are a good mind and the ability to think logically. But if theology is presented in story form, the meaning of the story cannot be fairly ascertained without becoming as much as possible a part of the culture of the storyteller and his or her listeners."[4]

4. Kenneth E. Bailey, *The Cross and the Prodigal: Luke 15 through the Eyes of Middle Eastern Peasants* (Downers Grove, IL: InterVarsity, 2005), 10.

How do Enlightenment-bound thinkers understand story? How do you think Western individualism, binary logic, and present-future utopian orientation to reality affect one's reading of the scriptures and understanding of theology? What could communal thinking and worldviews that are more comfortable with tension and mystery offer theological discussion and the scholarly community?

Mending the Hoop

A common way of viewing life in our Native American cultures is through a circle, a sacred circle or sacred hoop. The circle has no end or beginning; it is all-encompassing, and any point on the circle can be reached by anyone.

Our Aboriginal spiritual teachers speak of the reestablishment of the balance between human beings and the whole of creation as "mending the hoop." How can we come to a common truth of the history of White supremacy in order to deconstruct our own Western worldviews and to recognize the strength Indigenous people have to survive? What is the wisdom they have to contribute to reconcile us with the land by protecting it and restoring it? What does it mean to find a person who identifies as White as an ally, working against White supremacy to make reparations to Indigenous peoples and to go through a similar process with anyone else with whom it is needed? I believe this kind of spirituality must be demonstrated by vulnerability.

I believe the Creator to be the most vulnerable being who exists. If God is love, and love means being vulnerable, then God must represent the essence of vulnerability. The incarnation of Jesus expressed Great Mystery's vulnerability. Jesus's lifestyle of hanging out with the poor and the marginalized, empowering women, healing lepers, and so on expressed Creator's vulnerability. The crucifixion demonstrated God's vulnerability. Jesus radically expresses the most vulnerable Creator by coming from a shalom Trinity, sharing Creator's mission of love with us, and leaving the responsibility in our hands to co-act with God through love. God is in Jesus, and we, along with others who are different from us, are invited to become fellow human beings, to exchange and empower dignity in ourselves and in others, and to join in reciprocal conversations of each other's understanding of truth and how to live shalom with, for, and among the whole community of creation, including people. The opposite of vulnerability is control, including the illegitimate use of power. The illegitimate use of power via White supremacy and religious cultural hegemony, especially as used against others structurally, is among the primary failures of Western colonizer Christianity.

Structural change is needed now, but certain types of thinking are associated with change. There usually exists a wide gap between the people who set policy resulting in structural problems, and the people who are affected by such policy. Truly, those who are affected most—those who are expected to abide by the policy—must have genuine input in the process. This input, if authentic and empowered, turns into ownership at some point in the whole process. This wide gap exists for numerous reasons, including misunderstanding the role of power, or simply because of homeostasis, pragmatism, short-term thinking, someone's ego, or a lack of common experience. There are numerous ways that process can be circumvented or delegitimized. Systems tend to devolve and become corrupted over time. If structures don't remain pliable, they can become rigid and callous to those in the system. Any system's DNA is of primary importance. What I call the system's DNA is really about the intentions and processes when formulated. I think of DNA as an organizational atmosphere, vision, and process, not the actual rules or structure itself.

How to Make Change

An atmosphere that includes the following values can help foster long-term change:

- relationship-building, the most primary value
- trust-building, which requires consistent honesty and leads to loyalty
- humor, especially laughing at our weaknesses and mistakes
- equality, which means treating everyone fairly
- empowerment, which means allowing for innovation and advancement
- diversity of opinions, which means providing safe space for difference of thought without threat
- appreciation of individual giftings, which means allowing for difference, showing appreciation in tangible ways, and facing risky questions together, even if sometimes expressed as unruliness
- appreciation of out-of-the-box innovations, even when they are not a great success
- acceptance of both tradition and nontradition
- verifiable communication tools and devices; communication is key
- vulnerability and acceptance of our common humanity, which we call grace

Words have little to no value when Christian leaders are maintaining a corrupt system, even when it is not deliberate. Management can be an important role when everyone is content, but when there are concerns over basic human rights or justice or fairness, and so on, what we need to encourage is truth-telling. Unfortunately, dysfunctional systems have a way of disposing with truth-telling. The downward spiral from the system managers to the truth-tellers goes something like this:

- ignore and/or deny the concerns
- feign acceptance of the concerns
- pacify with good words and good intentions
- blame the messenger
- gather support for blame
- reject the messenger completely through ostracizing them or removing them

So, you must count the cost. If you want change, you must ask yourself if making change is worth it to you. Are the lives of Indigenous peoples or the cultural, religious, ethnic, racial, or gendered other worth it to you? Is the integrity of the gospel worth it to you? How about your own integrity?

Question and Response

What is the relationship between story and fact? For example, what is the relevance of the historical resurrection as it plays out in story?

As you know, among Native Americans there are different kinds of stories. We don't really classify them as true or not true when telling them. So, one of the mysteries is that you never quite know. You can be pretty sure when Indigenous people start talking about the animals all coming together for a council meeting that the story is not literally true, but there are also stories of our ancient beginnings and concerning our relationship with the Creator and our covenants. I think people would, if you press them, say those are fact. It's just that no one ever asks that question. It doesn't come up. Is that true or not? What's the difference if you get what's needed out of it?

The truth is in the story, whether it's fact or not fact. I don't know how to answer the question in terms of things like the resurrection. It's been sort of the Western obsession to prove the Bible, ever since the fundamentalist-progressive split. I think it could be an important question. I just don't think it's my question, and the reason it's not my personal question is because I have a relationship with Jesus, who is Spirit, and he talks to me and I talk to him. I wish he talked to me more often, but through lots of different ways he speaks. I have a relationship in the Spirit with Creator.

I talked about the story of the elder who was teaching all the medicine men and his having a relationship with Jesus to talk in the spirit, because Jesus is not here in the flesh, at least not literally. The Jesus I have conversations with is what makes sense when I read stories about him. Because that's what I'm feeling in my heart when I'm talking to Jesus. So I don't need to have someone ask, "Do you believe in the physical resurrection?" I can say, "Sure!" But it's just not my question. I don't know if that makes sense, and I know other people feel differently. I'm sure other Indigenous people feel differently. I'm coming from what I've observed from a traditional perspective. Fact and truth somehow are not my categories. It is, I guess, that truth overrides fact; maybe that's a way to say it.

I'm interested in Christian mission and how it has been part of the colonial project. What does mission look like in a world where those of us who are White don't want to extend the colonial project? Do we believe that it's good for all people to come to know Jesus?

Since I'm a missiologist, I hope I am prepared to answer that one. So I have these ten points I call "Woodley's Ten Missiological Imperatives," and they go something like this:

1. There is no place we can go where Jesus is not *already* present and active.

2. Since Jesus is active everywhere, the first responsibility of mission among any culture is not to teach, speak, or exert privilege but to discover what Jesus is doing in that culture.

3. Realize that God expects two conversions out of every missional encounter: (1) our conversion to the truths in

their culture and (2) their conversion to the truth we may bring to the encounter.

4. Our humility as dedicated servants of Jesus should naturally lead us to convert first to the truths in their culture, everywhere we see Jesus at work.

5. Through the work of culture guides (people of that culture), earnest study, prayer, and experiential failures, it is our responsibility to first adapt to and then embrace their culture and, as much as possible, their worldview.

6. Realize that conversion is both instantaneous and a process (the biblical idea of salvation as *becoming* wholly healed), and think through those implications as you begin to consider your time lines. Then, throw out your time lines.

7. During this time, also read, study, and discuss with others the ways that you can continue to deconstruct your own worldview and culture. This is a very long, painful, and yet freeing process.

8. Our own process of conversion may take years, so be patient with yourself and with God.

9. When and if they invite us to share the gospel they have noticed us living out, then the process formally known as cultural contextualization, or something like it, should occur, while always making it a priority to maintain everyone's dignity.

10. Their process of conversion may take years, if they ever do convert, but their conversion is not our business. Their conversion is their business, and it's only our concern if they choose to make it so.[5]

---

5. These are discussed more fully in Randy S. Woodley, "Mission and the Cultural Other: In Search of the Pre-colonial Jesus," *Missiology: An International Review* 43 (2015): 456–68.

When I use the word *conversion*, it's with a small *c*. Salvation in my understanding is a series of conversions and healings. My preferred word that captures salvation is *healing*, as healing is a process. We begin our healing, and we complete our healing, but we're also *being* healed. As Paul said, "Our salvation is nearer now than when we first believed" (Rom. 13:11). Part of that healing is decolonizing our own thinking and then, as much as possible, through the help of cultural guides, to indigenize ourselves to the other culture.

What's the difference between enculturating the gospel and syncretism? To put it in terms others might use, aren't you imposing Indigenous theology on the scriptures and somehow then polluting pure theology?

I also worry that it is a bit self-righteous of us to say that there's a pure theology and that it's ours. Unless we can live first-century Jewish lives in a Hellenized world, we're not going to be able to prevent imposing our own cultures on the scriptures. This question comes up often when we speak. One of the ways people ask it is, "How far is too far?" And my answer is always the same: It is not up to us to decide. That is up to that body to decide—the people who are dealing with the issue and who know their own culture well. It's not up to cultural interlopers, and I don't mean that in a derogatory way. But if we don't live in the culture or if we have a different worldview, we should at best be a junior partner in the process.

I knew a missionary to the Ikallahan people in the Philippines, and the whole village became followers of Christ in their own unique cultural ways. I was able to spend time with this missionary one day, and he's an older gentleman who was there for fifty or sixty years; he was eventually adopted as a tribal elder, but I asked him, I said, "What was the key for you?" He said, "I simply told the stories and I allowed them to theologize them. I trusted the Spirit to do the theologizing work." Maybe sometimes it doesn't work out, but I'm sure we don't have the right to impose our cultures on those cultures who are trying to figure it out.

Western civilization has dramatically changed in the last twenty or thirty years. Is there really a unified Western worldview? Many people, even in Indigenous communities, are affected by the advent of virtual reality, which itself is removed from the notion of the land. International corporations are in many ways the colonizers of the present, are they not?

So, in New York City they say, "From your lips to God's ears." I wish that this scenario you painted was so. I think it's easy for us to think like this when we're in advanced educational settings, like seminaries and universities, to assume that things have all changed for the better. In the United States what I'm talking about is still very common. I think that it is so ubiquitous that there are these hidden snakes that we must find that are still there, that we might overlook, that'll come back and bite us if we don't continue to dig in the same holes, so to speak. I do think, yes, things are changing a bit, but I don't think they're changing as much as your question might suggest, or at least that's not my experience. But I am conscious that my own experience is very different from young people coming into this historic moment.

The advent of the virtual nature of culture, the interconnectivity across and breaking down of cultural barriers, makes me wonder if there is an opportunity to better reflect what's in our global phenomena. America itself is run by a collection

of international corporations, so how does that affect where we are?

I teach like you do, probably to a lot of millennials, and they don't want the same paradigm that their parents had. They want a whole different paradigm. They don't want the same church. They want something different. They're looking for different things, but they also identify readily with the things that I'm talking about, because that Western worldview is what they grew up under, and that's exactly what they don't want anymore. So I'm hopeful. I also believe that many of those corporations hold the same Western values that I've been talking about, so we're still dealing with the same animal, so to speak. It just looks different.

Does there not have to be some dualism in any society, because wherever there is a sense of evil, there has to be a sense of the good?

That's a little different from the kind of dualism that I'm talking about. I'm talking about the specific Platonic dualism that says that we must invest ourselves more in the ethereal or spiritual, the products of the mind, over and above the body, the material world. So, do I think we have to have dualism? No, not the kind I'm talking about. Just because there are two things that seem to be opposites doesn't mean that it is Platonic dualism.

We don't talk a lot about humor in the church or in Christian discussions of spirituality, yet it was one of the key points in the harmony way. Could you say a little bit more about what we can learn and how we can bring that into our Christian spirituality?

At our powwows, a long time ago, we actually had clowns that were part of the powwows, and the clowns would do silly things. It was kind of like the modern rodeos. Our emcees are only good if they keep people laughing all the time. Usually, the jokes are at the expense of somebody else, as most First Nations have very self-deprecating humor. I have been around White folks and tried to show Native movies or Native humor. The question that constantly comes up is why they're talking about such terrible things! How can they laugh about these things? Maybe that's just a Native characteristic or that's something for oppressed peoples, but if you can't laugh at it, then you're going to die from it! So you must be able to laugh at even the worst circumstances and be able to see something funny in it. Something humorous creates part of that balance of life and in a lot of our ceremonies.

We have funny kinds of humor. I have led sweat lodge for the last thirty years, and one of the things I was taught was that if it gets to be too intense and people are just drained from all the serious heart talk and things, you take the fourth round and you make jokes or you tell funny stories to balance things out. I remember one time I was at a Hopi Bean Dance, and we were up on the top of the buildings overlooking the plaza, and they had Kasharis, these clowns that went around and they talked to the dancers who were in line. And there was this one Kashari who was telling this guy off, and everybody around was laughing. We didn't speak Hopi, so I asked my Hopi friend what he was saying. He said, "He's kind of shaming him, but it's funny. He's saying, 'Hey, you're supposed to be such an upright person and faithful to your wife, but why is it on Friday nights after midnight we see your truck parked behind widow so-and-so's house?'" Everybody thought that was hilarious, him getting outed right in front of everybody. We have our own kinds of humor.

Some humor is scheduled in ceremony, and if it's not, it will be unscheduled. The thing that surprises non-Native folks the most is when they come and hang out with Indigenous people. They say, "I can't believe you guys laugh so much and have such a good time." You know, I just think that's part of a survival mechanism, but it's certainly built into our value system now.

I'm wondering how much decolonization is needed among Indigenous millennials. Are you finding that they want to decolonize and discover their identity?

I attended a workshop in 1991 held, as I recall, by the University of New Mexico called "Violence, Abuse, and Neglect among North American Natives." In that national study they did a number of things to discover who were the most affected by violence and abuse and neglect, and they were able to create three categories of measurement. One category was the very traditional Native who lived on the reservation. The next was the people who lived off the reservation, mostly in cities.[6] This category of people are those who participate in Native American events and in social gatherings, maybe at the city's Native Center, or they travel to their reservations. Those people's kids might dance in powwows, and they try to keep one foot in the culture. The third category are those who are completely assimilated to the colonizing culture; they understand themselves to be Native in name only.

Of these three categories, violence, neglect, and abuse was highest in the third category, and in the first category it was the lowest. Colonization just doesn't work well on our Native people.

6. About 70 percent of our Native people in the United States live in cities. Joe Whittle, "Most Native Americans Live in Cities, Not Reservations," *The Guardian*, September 4, 2017, https://www.theguardian.com/us-news/2017/sep/04/native -americans-stories-california.

Take away our culture and our roots and often we're left with nothing. Then we try to fix it with all kinds of Western remedies. There are young people who have gone through various stages of seeking a more traditional identity, and then moving away from it. It is one of the dilemmas that Native people face, because we have the pressure in a colonized society and there's a difficult choice for them to make. Many of us are constantly having to define and re-define our identity. We are all struggling with identity problems because of modernity and colonization. I do come across a lot of young people who want to become re-Indigenized, so to speak. Often they were adopted, or maybe their parents were urbanized. But there are a lot of young people out there who want to be Indigenous or at least discover what that means. We've got a whole lifetime to learn, and people can make decisions at different times in their lives. But we want to be there for people who are ready.

How do we work to effect change as settlers, or as those who are privileged and seeking to walk alongside marginalized people?

I like movements that grow from the ground up because it gives more people a chance to participate. I think the process will always turn around and bite you if decisions are made from the top down. So, we have a problem in the United States because, for example, a group of people of color will want to change an unjust system, but the people who are in charge, who are generally White, just want to improve the system. They want to make it better. That process doesn't seem to work well for people of color. Everyone may think, well, because they have good hearts and good intentions it will work, but what they don't understand about that system is that the system, even if you improve it, is still not made for people of color; it was constructed for White people. That means that people of color have to be at the table to create a new system, and that's a really painful process for institutions. It means letting many of your old assumptions die and coming up with new models. Because if the old DNA is still there, it'll manifest itself eventually.

When two people have a child, the only DNA that person receives are from those two parents. In an organization, if you want a different DNA, you must introduce different parents in order to create a different kind of child. That's the best way I can explain liberation theology. It is basically a process in which many different people are involved in creating that new system or paradigm. Of course, some would argue that this is exactly what Jesus did.

Are there places in our communities where they are ready for the decolonization process? Do you think storytelling would benefit Western minds as much in the process?
I think we're all in this together. When I talk about decolonization, I'm talking about all of us. When I talk about Indigenization, I'm talking about all of us doing this together. I always hesitate to say "save our world," because I think the earth is going to be okay, but maybe we're not going to be around to see that if we don't do something together—it has to be done together. I think now we're in a countdown stage, and we've got to do this together or it's not going to get done. So, we all need each other. I think there's nothing like common oppression to bring people together, but hopefully, relationships will develop so our common oppression is not all that's holding our efforts together.

How do you recommend we operate in such a consumeristic culture where we are so disconnected from the most foundational things like where our food comes from?

I'm against consumerism. The permaculture communities are doing a lot to empower non-consumeristic alternatives. They are active and really fired up, and they're doing all kinds of things: urban permaculture, rural permaculture, and CSAs (Community Supported Agriculture). We have had the privilege of hanging around with some of them, and we try to learn from them. They sometimes forget to give a nod and a wink to the Indigenous practices they are doing, but a lot of what they are doing in working with nature is what our Indigenous people have done before. Get involved in a local permaculture group and start doing something with them, and you'll get excited by being outside, learning, and growing stuff. At some point I'm pretty sure our US economy is going to fail, and at some point, that may mean our survival begins to depend on these skills, so it'd be good to have those skills now and be ready.

Closing Interview

A continuation of the Red Couch Conversation.

Do you think that Western culture is causing this sense of people not knowing who they are? And then our sense of meaning becomes lost because we've lost touch with the land? Or is it far more complicated than that?

Well, there's probably a lot of things involved, even just the concerns of globalization. But I think a lot of it has to do with modernity and how we have lost touch with the land, especially those of us who have been colonized, and our families are colonized. Those who have not made the choices along the way and who never wanted to make those changes. It becomes very disruptive. I think when you decide to make changes for yourself and move, that's the settler colonial pattern. It's very different from you having to make these changes regardless of whether you want them or not. I think it does something different to people's identities and to their theologies, and so in the Western world, you adopt a more universal theology. This universal theology is supposed to be good for all people at all times because you don't have a place to connect it to. Whereas with our Indigenous people, there is a local theology based on the land, and it's based on the stories that come out of that land. That Indigenous worldview and theology is based on the ceremonies that are practiced on that land, and it's based on the community that, at one time, was fairly intact. Not perfect, but fairly intact. And I think that detachment from the land has created two different theologies. Two different theologies and two different worldviews. I don't think we can talk about theology without talking about worldview.

Just to make sure that no one misinterprets me, I'm all about our people finding agency. The goal of the church and the goal of the government was to take away our Indigenous agency and create dependency, so that we would be dependent on them. Sometimes when we start talking about what has happened to Native people, it's really easy for people to think, "Oh, the poor Indigenous people, you know, we feel sorry for them," but that is not where I'm going with this. Where I'm going is that we need to actually create agency, both in Native people and in Western folks too.

To what degree can we any longer even talk about a Western worldview?

There obviously are lots of variations of a Western worldview, but the particular Western worldview that I'm talking about, I believe, is the dominant historical worldview that has been widely held among White folks who feel superior to Native folks. It comes through Greece and Rome and Anglo-Saxonism, and basically, at least in the United States, it permeates everything. So *that* Western worldview I would call both classist and racist, and I can say that historically, this is fact.

For some, the Western worldview feels fragmented and leads to a real sense of disorientation—we don't know who we are

or what the church is here for. Some of us recognize the bankruptcy of the colonial project, and we still want to be Jesus-followers. How do we do that in authentic ways that acknowledge where we've come from but also give us hope for the future, rather than a sometimes-pervasive sense of meaninglessness? Can Indigenous theology help us?

First, allow me to say that some of my Indigenous friends would say that Indigenous theology is an oxymoron. Part of the Western academic project is to separate and categorize. For example, separating practical theology from theology proper, if you think about it, is ridiculous. So an Indigenous influence can play a role in bringing them back together because, in our Indigenous worldview, there is no separation between heart and mind; instead, there is constant integration. This is one of the reasons I hesitate to call myself a theologian, by the way, because does that then mean that I'm not a farmer, or does that mean I'm not an artist, or can we all be different and the same intersecting together? So all of these are extrinsic categories that bind us to established categories in the Western mind.

There are some wonderful things about the Western worldview. This ability to create extrinsic categories and examine them so precisely can be a really good thing. Think about it like this: as a person with peripheral neuropathy, I'm glad I have a podiatrist and a neurologist and a general practitioner. But if one of those treats me as if I'm just a foot, then I'm in trouble. The problem is that we begin to take these categories, and we live them out as if they are the whole of reality. Reality is bringing them all back together. Theology (proper) is only as good as practical theology. Our philosophy is only as good as how much it serves the common good. The extrinsic categories, the products of the mind if you will, are pervasive in Platonic dualism, and they end up being elevated to the point where we can't put Humpty Dumpty together again. As a result, we put our faith in our beliefs, we put our faith in our doctrines, we put our faith in our church covenants, we put our faith in the written Word of God, we put our faith in our constitutions, and so on. In the West, all of these become sacrosanct because they are products of the mind.

In a system based on this kind of dualism, what we actually do becomes less important than what we believe. As Indigenous people are becoming more and more fragmented, all the time becoming more susceptible to the kinds of colonial patterns that have beset everyone else, we're losing that holistic worldview. This era we are experiencing now may be the last opportunity for us all to regain our soul, if you will. I think this is especially true as we are losing our traditional elders. I don't understand myself as an elder, like the ones from whom I learned. I feel more like an elder-junior. I'm not someone who people should be listening to and saying, "Oh, he's an elder, and so you should listen to everything he says." I don't consider myself an expert, but I am, I think, a good observer, and I have some pretty good intuition, and I think that we need some big, big changes in our world. So listening not just to Indigenous theologians but to Indigenous people in general, especially traditional elders who have been living these values all of their lives, is the most important thing we can do to help us to regain our souls as Indigenous people.

How can we help students and help people in churches to open up to a different worldview? Do we have to provide experiences? Can it be done through thought exercises?

I think you must provide experiences, yes. I've been running a sweat lodge for over thirty years and have hosted some hardcore White folks, people who we would consider "double-White"

folks, European descended folks who exhibit all the characteristics of the privilege of Whiteness. They have come to visit our
sweat lodge, and their whole lives have been changed in one
night. I think it's because they've not had the opportunity to
experience a whole expression of their faith or their spirituality up until that point. The structures that they've been living
in, as followers of Jesus, as Christians, have not provided that
experience of wholeness for them. It behooves educational institutions, and anybody associated with the church really, to
provide those kinds of experiences. People need to live through
something that's a whole experience, as opposed to just those
products of the mind.

A woman came up to me recently and said, "You know,
there's a lot of people going to Eastern spirituality and Celtic
spirituality and other practices like that. What do you think
about that? How does that fit in your paradigm?" Calmly, I said,
"Well, you know we're all Indigenous from somewhere, right?" I
love to see European folks connecting with their own Indigenous
spiritualities because there's so much there! My presumption
is that similar things happened to the Celts, for example, that
happened to our Native American people. The church made up
stories and lies to destroy those spiritualities. They condemned
them as evil and of the devil. There's a path to discovery, and
sometimes it is a very long path to finally get to the point of
conversion. I think that anything in a person's experience that
helps them begin to deconstruct their own Western worldview
and realize that there's another way of being in the world that's
not based simply on intellectual assent, is a good thing. This
often means that they have to have a different experience.

**But how would you encourage people to embrace the ex-
perience, given that people are often afraid to encounter**

something different, like a sweat lodge? What happens at a sweat lodge is so outside our realm of experience. How do we encourage people to understand the encounter without judging first, and yet still be seen as followers of Jesus? I think it's okay to let go because Jesus has me, so I can explore, and it's exciting and fun. But some people feel very threatened by that, and I sympathize with them.

I think perhaps one of the first steps is deciding that you just can't be in control anymore. Most of the Western social systems are built around control. I wrote an article in our first issue of *Journal of NAIITS*, back in 2003, comparing structure and values in the Indigenous church or Indigenous traditions with those in the Christian church, and I found that everything is so very opposite.[1] So, we start with when a person first goes in the church, and what happens? Where do the children go? Where do we sit? Is it okay to get up during the service? The expectations are so opposite our Indigenous ceremonies. You can't look at that from an Indigenous perspective without asking, "Why is everyone trying to control everyone else?" Even the way that we face the front, if you still have pews, you are facing the back of everyone's head! What does that say about what you think about the priesthood of all believers if only the person that is in front has control of everyone? So our Native values grate against that kind of order and control.

I think letting go of that control is part of the healing. To say that I don't need to be afraid. I don't have to worry about it! I mean, what's the worst that can happen if you just let loose? So people must figure out a way to "let go and let God," as the old adage goes, and actually do it.

1. Randy Woodley, "Hard Questions concerning Structure and Values in the New North American Aboriginal Church," *Journal of NAIITS* 1 (2003): 67–71.

You mentioned oral tradition and telling stories. You mentioned that the Bible should have been told, not written for Indigenous people. Can you speak a little more to this?

I was a pastor for seven years in Carson City, Nevada. Most of our congregation were traditional folks, meaning they didn't come from a church background but rather from a traditional tribal background. I couldn't get some of them to read the scriptures, but when I would translate the scriptures in a more contextual way that they could relate to, they would often ask me afterward, "Can I get a copy of that?" So I suggested to them that we should have a class to teach the Bible, so they could see that these authors were brown people who were more Indigenous than Western. We did, and as the course went on, they pressed the question of who translated all this from the original languages. And of course, the translation committees were almost all White folks, mostly White men, who translated these things, and the class said, "See, the White man wrote the Bible!"

As Indigenous people, we have the history of White men writing things down, because we have stacks of treaties that have not been kept throughout American history. In the United States they say we've had over eight hundred treaties that are proven to not have been kept! Things written down are viewed with suspicion, or even ignored, as a result of the lies that have been told about what's been written down. So they said the White men who translated the Bible probably kept stuff out that they didn't want us to know, and they put things in that they did want us to know that weren't there originally. So in some circles there is little trust that the scriptures are in the best interest of Indigenous people. That's when I began to wrestle with all this. The scriptures were oral before they were written. And we don't have the original oral content of the

Aramaic-speaking Jesus. What we have are copies of orality in the Greek. I personally am not so sure that I buy into the belief that it is sacred because it is written.

I understand that I might be wrong. I have a friend, Ray Aldred, who often when he speaks, he reads the passage and says, "Just listen to the story." Don't get hung up on the fact that everything's chaptered and numbered in the way someone else saw it, but listen to the story. We might say, listen to the context. Listen to the story. We must understand the story before we can understand the scriptures. So to me it's the story that becomes important. The background story and those words that are informing the story.

Do you think that the traditional cultures of Indigenous peoples are more in line with the story of the Bible and peoples of the Bible? Is the divide thinner from Indigenous cultures to the cultural expressions of the Bible?

When we were first doing this work twenty-five or thirty years ago among our Native people and saying that it's okay to be Native and follow Jesus, what became known as the Native American cultural contextual movement, this concern would often come up.[2] They would ask it like, "How far is too far?" "Where's the line?" "Where do you cross the line?" So I used to say, "Well, you (as outsiders) don't get to decide that for them. Only the people in their context get to decide that for themselves."[3] Now, I believe very much in there being both an inside and an outside perspective, what we call the emic

2. See, for example, the conversations had in the inaugural volumes of the *Journal of NAIITS* (2003).

3. For one example of this discussion, see Casey Church, "Creating Native American Expressions of Christian Faith: More Than the Looks on Their Faces," *Journal of NAIITS* 12 (2014): 45–62.

and etic perspectives in anthropology. There is the insider, who knows the culture well, and the outsider, who knows other cultures well, but it's the community that gets to decide. It's not the outsiders coming in and saying, "Here's how the Bible is supposed to be interpreted." I think, in the end, if we don't own our own stories, then they're not our stories.

The Jerusalem Council in Acts 15 issued one of the most important decisions that the church would ever make. "Can the gentiles receive the gospel?" You know there were all kinds of folks vying for all kinds of positions there in the discussion, but the list of those four things was very simple, and they all had to do with not going back into idol worship and to promote the fellowship and unity of the community across ethnic lines.[4] Don't eat meat sacrificed to idols, meat of strangled animals, or blood, and avoid the immoral temple prostitution. But I think about if some of our august theological bodies would have been asked the same question: we would have met for six years and come up with a list of thirty things that have to be done. But in Acts 15 it says that the whole church agreed on these things (Acts 15:22, 25).

The council letter seems to show a level of trust in the gentiles to come up with their own understanding, but with a little guidance. I think that kind of trust is a model for us as we go to our local communities and our local tribes and different people. Let's tell them the stories and let them do the theologizing.

Another way we need help is in engaging our local Indigenous communities. Many of us growing up didn't even know there were Indigenous communities, let alone where they were.

4. David K. Strong, "The Jerusalem Council: Some Implications for Contextualization," in *Mission in Acts: Ancient Narratives in Contemporary Context*, ed. R. L. Gallagher and P. Hertig (Maryknoll, NY: Orbis Books, 2004), 196–208.

This has changed somewhat, but in many places there is still little contact between Indigenous and settler communities. Some of us are very hesitant to re-enact old patterns of being. How do we as Christians engage with, for example, Indigenous ritual that we may not be sure about? How would you advise us on things like that?

I used to visit an old Comanche Baptist pastor named Robert when I was a commissioned missionary with the American Baptists. He was in Lawton, Oklahoma. A ninety-three-year-old man who pastored this Baptist church for the past fifty years. He went to residential boarding school, and he was given his name there. He had lived a long time, a long life living in both worlds. I was shocked one day when he said to me, "Randy, do you know how at a powwow we have our giveaways, and you know, when a Native person receives something, they just shake your hand and say, 'thank you'? You ever notice how White people just go overboard with thanks? They thank you all day, and it may not even be a great gift, but they just want to thank you and thank you to make sure you know." Then he got quiet and he said, "You know why that is?" I responded, "No."

"I'll tell you why, it's because White people, deep down inside, don't want to be indebted to an Indian for anything!" And I think until that dynamic is dealt with, the idea that you might make a mistake should not be the concern. Your concern is that you need to be corrected by the people from whom you are trying to learn. That is a big threshold in the United States. I don't know about Canada, but in the United States everybody is afraid to do the wrong thing. I think about that story Robert told me because after ninety-three years of living in two worlds, White and Indian, this is what he ended up with. It's kind of sad. This is where he ends up in his understanding of what's going on between settler folks and First Nations. I think it's this "letting loose" of the control where one is afraid to be corrected when things go wrong. So the question becomes, "Am I willing to risk making mistakes in order to establish the relationship? Am I willing to be corrected by an Indian enough to take the risk?"

I was part of a men's group for many years, and we called it "the no BS zone." We were a group of sixty to seventy men, consisting predominantly of African Americans and Whites, who would meet weekly. There were also a few people like me and my friend Richard Twiss and a couple other people from various ethnicities. One day someone asked me, "Why do you keep coming back here?" I realized at that point, the reason I kept coming back is because the White guys kept coming back. I had decided that I would keep coming back because they don't have to come. Everything's going to be fine for them if they don't come, but we must come back if things are going to change, and so that's why I attended. As long as the White guys were willing to stay at the table, I was willing as well. I always tell White people, "You have to be at the table, and you must stay at the table, no matter how bad things get, no matter how sad the stories get, no matter how angry you get or we get. Remember, you're making the choice to be at the table so that things can change." So it really behooves White folks to stay at the table to make those mistakes. When you don't understand the dynamics, show up anyway. Try to figure it out and trust the process even when you are afraid of it. You know, it's natural to be afraid of what we don't know or what we don't understand. It's going to be challenging, but just keep being present because you have a choice to be absent, but then nothing will likely change.

One of the main aspects of a Western worldview is individualism. That ties in with how we understand ourselves and how we exist as human beings in community. I can't help but think that there is help that can come from Indigenous worldviews and perspectives.

I think we can come together when we have common values. Sometimes those values are good; sometimes they're not so good. So we have a group in the United States that call themselves the Ku Klux Klan. I hear they like to hang out together, but their values aren't so good. When we build around good values, what some people might call the "common good" and when those values are clear, good community can happen.

In the third lecture I talked a bit about my dissertation project, which deals with ten Indigenous values that I've been able to identify. Those ten values are pretty clearly aligned with the scriptures. When we live according to those values in proximity to one another, we have a real opportunity to become community. It's not complicated. In the United States, where I believe we're even more of an individualized culture than up here in Canada, the individualism really disrupts our spirituality tremendously. We understand everything, for example in the scriptures, as about me, not about us, and it deteriorates the community. I can't help but think that whether it's good values or bad values, it's important to understand that human beings are not just about me but that as a human being *I* am an *us*! We are an *us* even when we're alone. I always tell people, "If you're in creation, you are not alone; you're in a community." You may not speak the same language as the rest of the beings around you, but they are there, and they understand your presence. We are never alone.

Is there a language that we should use besides the language of "the common good"? Some people see the language of

common good as colonial in its expression. Who determines what the common good is? And who belongs to the "common" in the common good? Are there ways that we can still talk about what is good for everybody, or will it always be established by a White person from a colonial worldview?

The question of who gets to decide that is more important to me. If the community doesn't get to decide that, then it's not the common good. We must always be careful about the process. The process is more important than the result, just like I believe pedagogy is more important than content. Sometimes we must become almost entirely disenfranchised so we understand what the common good looks like. We need to be honest about what we bring to the table and the baggage we bring, the influence we bring, and all those kinds of things.

I'm wondering about how in a disconnected, contemporary culture, it seems that as human beings we're meant to have ways of marking out stages of life in community, where together it's acknowledged that a person is now an adult, or it's acknowledged that a person is struggling, and the community indicates its support. Could you comment on the importance of ritual and the challenge this perhaps brings to a Western worldview and to Western churches?

One of the greatest things they teach in anthropology about ritual process is that you are in line for conversion when you're at the status quo, and then there's something that causes you to delve into liminality.[5] So now you're in this liminal stage and depending on what happens during this time and the decisions you make, you come out different, and you find a new status quo. So, in a way, ceremony is basically a way of creating

5. Roger D. Abrahams, Victor Turner, and Alfred Harris, *The Ritual Process: Structure and Anti-structure* (1969; repr., New York: Routledge, 1995).

liminality. This is how, as I understand it, we can renew ourselves. A lot of those ceremonies, especially coming-of-age ceremonies, have been taken out of the Western culture, and things like getting your driver's license have replaced them.

I think about one of my Maasai friends who's from the Samburu area in Kenya. Among other things, Michael had to kill a lion when he was a teenager in order to become a man, which is about as extreme as I can think of—obviously every culture is different. There are different ways of doing ceremony, and I don't know exactly what has caused the West to abandon their ceremonies. A lot of things happened in church history that have created disdain for symbols, and perhaps the Protestant reaction to Catholic liturgies and symbols has fostered this rejection. But we still have our symbols. I used to have a reoccurring argument with a fundamentalist Baptist pastor about the use of Native American symbols, and I would point out the fact that he has gold around his Bible, which doesn't make it more precious, but it is symbolic. He bows his head and closes his eyes to pray, and he holds hands with others or lays hands on others to pray. Those are all symbolic gestures. We use symbolism constantly because symbolism is communication.

I think there's perhaps a fear that if we create too much of a disruption in life, it may inconvenience people. Our own children had young-man and young-woman ceremonies to come into that next phase of their life. Because our communities have been so disrupted, it was impossible to do either a Cherokee or Shoshone ceremony, and so we combined them with a couple other aspects to do their coming-of-age ceremonies. One of the borrowed aspects we used when my youngest son was coming into his young-man years came at the very end of his ceremony. We had sweat lodge and we had elders and others speaking to him, a time when the men spoke alone with him, and a time when the women spoke alone with him. At the conclusion, we had him run down the road as hard as he could to the end of the road. The idea was to run off his childhood and to walk back and to think about what everyone had said over the past few days. To think about what it means to be a young man. As he walked back, the community was standing at the end of the road to embrace him and congratulate him. I remember it meaning so much to both him and us and the whole community. They were invested in him walking in a different way than he did as a child. I think people are going to have to come up with their own ceremonies. Maybe they can borrow from others with the right permissions.

I recall another very powerful time when Edith and I were asked to take part in a "Wiping Away Tears" ceremony for combat veterans to heal. The particular tribe that was doing this had asked the Nez Perce tribe if they could borrow one of their ceremonies, so they met with them and all agreed. This ceremony was for veterans who had come back from the war who were experiencing PTSD and who had never dealt with it in a good way. We have ways in our Native community to deal with those things, and this is one of them. The veterans lined up. They brought water from their homes, which was supposed to represent their tears. All those were poured together in a bucket. When they came through the line, they dipped their hands in red paint, which symbolized the blood that they had shed and the things that they had done to take human life or contribute to shedding blood. Then they would come down to Edith and me, and we would wash the paint off their hands. They would then be prayed over by elders. We saw all these grown men, elders, and others who would break down crying because it was such a powerful symbol. These chains of guilt that have held them for so long were now gone. There are so many good reasons for having ceremony. I think we need a lot more of it, and the West has to figure out what's important to them so that they can have healing too.

Perhaps one of the problems is the idea that we're okay, and therefore we don't need things like this. I know that there's a longing for it, and I think that if we look at the rituals, the traditional rituals—for example, baptism ceremony or Eucharist—we've so individualized these things as to almost lift them out of community.

Absolutely! That's what 1 Corinthians 11 is about. The background is that the wealthy people are getting there early and eating all the food while the poor people and slaves have to work and are coming in later, so they don't have any food, and they are the ones who really need it. When the apostle Paul says, "Examine yourselves" (1 Cor. 11:28 NRSV), we take that to mean examine the whole body, examine yourselves. Are you treating people around you unequally? But we've taken that to mean, Do I have any sins in my life that are unconfessed? which is just a smidgeon of what that passage is actually about. Are we missing the profound significance of sharing the bread and sharing the cup together and the unity this brings? This passage is about the called-out ones celebrating a meal together in equity and equality. This is in the context of Jesus's teachings on shalom.

Index

Adam, 57, 59
Africans, 95, 132
Alexandria, Egypt, 100n3
Alfred, Gerald Taiaiake, 14–15
Anglo-Saxon, 21, 23, 34, 120
anthropocentrism, 73, 100–101
Arensberg, Conrad, 65
Asbury Seminary, 94–95
atheists, Native, 51
Australia, 71, 95

Bailey, Kenneth, 102
balance. *See* harmony and balance
Baptists, 5, 89, 128, 132
Baum, L. Frank, 70n12
Bears, 54–55
beliefs, 61–62
Beringia land bridge, 26
Bible. *See* scripture
Blue Hole spring, 16
Boston Colony, 64
Bradford, William, 33–34
Brown, Brian Edward, 67–68
Brueggemann, Walter, 66, 91, 95

Budden, Christopher, 71
Bushnell, David, 33

Cahokia, 28–29, 31
Canada, 10, 22, 130
    Indigenous people's poverty, 15–16
    Truth and Reconciliation Commis-
        sion, 16–17
categorization, 72–73, 77–78, 99,
    121–22
    reality and, 63–64, 99–100
Celts, 123
ceremonies, 16, 22, 59, 92–94, 120,
    124
    coming of age, 131–33
    healing, 133–34
    humor, 113–14
    Indigenous narrative theology, 62,
        120
    rituals, 128–29, 131–32, 134
Chaco Canyon, 29, 31
Cherokees, 2–5, 86, 90, 132
    Bears, 54–55
    Chickamaugan, 2, 17–18

Grandmother Turtle, 38–41
harmony, 67–68
land misuse, 54–57
religion, 69–70
Selu and Kanati, 59
Tellico, 15–16
United Keetoowah Band, OK, 14
Christianity/Christians, 50, 104
empire and, 44–45
Indigenous people and, 44–45, 98
Indigenous religion and, 12–13
mission, 33–36, 64–65, 108–10, 128
noncontradiction, law of, 63–64
Churchill, Winston, 14
Clay, Henry, 34–35
colonization, 33–36, 50–51, 64–65, 72
disease and, 31–32
genocide, 16, 33–36, 70
Great Commission and, 35, 45–46
identity, 114–15, 119–20
of place, 60–61
settlers, 32, 42–43, 53–54, 81–82,
128–29
Columbus, Christopher, 26–27, 33
Comanche, 128
common good, 121–22, 130–31
community, 83–87, 93, 101, 126–27,
130–33
Community of Creator, 49–50, 86–87
conquest, worldview of, 62–63,
64–65, 70–72
Constantinian Empire, 44–45, 100–101
contextualization, 100n3, 109
control, 79, 82–83, 101–2, 104, 124
of Native peoples, 33, 72, 128–29
conversion, 108–10, 123
creation, 65–68, 94
Genesis account, 57, 59, 84, 96–97
harmony, 68–70

learning from, 76–77
narratives, 57–58, 68
Creator, 10, 38, 40–41, 56, 74
Community of, 49–50, 86–87
creation and, 57–59, 66–67, 86–87
Great Mystery, 72, 80, 92, 103
Jesus as, 48–49, 68–69
Sun and, 47–48
vulnerability, 103–4
culture/cultures, 108–9, 110–12, 131
Aboriginal/Indigenous, 37, 50,
102–3, 114–15, 126–27
American, 2–3, 83, 130
Anglo-Saxon, 21, 23, 34, 120
Greco-Roman, 21, 23, 60, 84, 98,
120
Greek, 21–22, 23, 26
Indigenous Cosmopolitan, 3–4
mound-building, 28–29, 31
stomp dance, 5, 47–48
Western, 79–80, 119, 132
Cyprian, 100n3

Dakota Access Pipeline, 81
David, King, 63
decolonization, 15, 43, 91, 114–15,
116
democracy, 22, 100–101
disappearing Indian, myth of, 16,
34–36
disease, 31–32, 55–56, 78
disruptive ideas, 9
diversity, 4, 27, 49–50, 87, 94–95,
105
Doctrine of Discovery, 30–31, 35,
45, 97
Douglas, Kelly Brown, 23
dreams, 22, 56, 61

drought, 31
drug use, 5–6, 11
dualism, 45, 63–64, 98, 99–100, 112,
    121–22
  theological, 72–73

education, 1–2, 4–5, 14–15, 22–23,
    42, 111, 123
  of history, 25–30
  seminary, 89–90, 94–95
elders, 51–52, 122
  respect for, 11–12, 41, 81
  teaching of, 10–11, 37, 91, 132–33
eloheh, 67–68, 91–92
Eloheh Indigenous Center for Earth
    Justice, 2
Emerson, Michael, 73–74
empowerment, 36–37, 105
Enlightenment, the, 46, 72–73, 84,
    103
equality, 63, 100, 105, 134
Eucharist, the, 134
Europeans, 15, 27, 31–32, 41–43
  colonization, 31–32, 70, 72, 97
  theology, 62, 71
  worldview, 41–42, 71, 101, 122–23
evangelism, 45–46, 85. *See also*
    missions
Eve, 59
evil, 80, 102, 112
exodus story, 46–47
experience, 10, 57, 92, 111
  knowledge and, 61–62, 67, 71
  truth and, 62–63, 92
  worldview and, 122–24

faith, 59–60, 66, 122, 123
Fanon, Frantz, 15n5

farming/gardening, 6–7, 59, 117
  Native seeds, 1, 6–7, 27, 59
  permaculture, 75, 117
food/food systems, 27–28, 59, 75–76,
    117
forgiveness, 51–52

Ganesh and Kartikeya, 58–59
genetics, American Indians, 32
genocide, 16, 33–36, 70
gospel, the, 45, 59–60, 95–96, 109
  enculturating, 110–11
Great Commission, 35, 45–46
Great Migration, 3–4
Great Mystery, 72, 80, 92, 103
Greco-Roman, 21, 23, 60, 84, 98,
    120
Greek culture/civilization, 21–22,
    23, 26

harmony and balance, 62–63, 68–70,
    79–80, 85–86
  Cherokee view, 67–68
  as circular, 63, 92, 103
  human responsibility, 48, 58, 60,
    68–70, 86
  shalom, 68–70, 71–72, 85–87, 95–97,
    98–103, 134
  truth and, 71–72
  the way of, 90–95
Hayward Lectures, 9
healing, 69, 72–73, 79, 110, 124
  song, 19–20
  veterans, 133–34
history, 25–30
  church, American, 26–27
  interpretation of, 23–25
  land and, 66–68

pre-colonial, 25–30
theology and, 14–17
Hohokum, 26, 29–30
holistic worldview, 62, 75–76, 98–99, 122
Hopi, 113
hospitality/generosity, 33, 51, 94
host people, recognizing, 10–12, 41
House of Freedom Caucus, 22
human fallibility, 50, 51–52, 71, 79
humor, 93, 98, 105, 112–14

identity, 2–5, 10–11, 13–14, 94
colonization and, 114–15, 119–20
Ignatius of Antioch, 100
Ikallahan people (Philippines), 95, 110–11
incarnation, 49, 87, 103–4
Indigenous Cosmopolitanism, 3–4
individualism, 61, 73–74, 79, 83–84, 101, 103, 130

Jacobs, Adrian, 37
Jerusalem Council, 127
Jesus Christ, 5–6, 51, 67
as Creator, 48–49, 68–69
following, 44–46, 51–52, 60, 107–8
history, interpretation of, 23–25
incarnation, 49, 87, 103–4
Indigenous people and, 11–13, 44, 74
redemption, 79
resurrection, 107–8
stories, teaching, 84–86, 97
working of, 108–9
worldview, 46, 73
Jones, Evan, 90

Keetoowah tradition, 1
stomp dance culture, 5, 47–48
United Keetoowah Band, OK, 14
Kennedy, John F., 17
Kenya, 95, 132
King, Martin Luther, Jr., 16
Kodiak, Alaska, 25, 89

land, 53–57, 58, 61, 64–65, 96–97
disconnection from, 103, 119–20
history and, 66–68
misuse of, 54–57
place, theology of, 65–68, 120
stealing, 64, 71
theology, 58, 65–68
universalizing, 60–61
welcome, 9–10, 54
liminality, 131–32
listening, 41–42, 57, 71, 76–77, 126

Maasai, 95, 132
Manifest Destiny, 35, 97
Mann, Charles, 30
Maori, 72, 95
marginalized people, 71, 87, 96–97
materialism, consumerism, 102, 117
Mather, Cotton, 34, 64
medicine, 27, 56, 78
memorializing, 43, 82
Midewiwin Lodge, 11–12
millennials, 112, 114–15
mission, Christian, 33–36, 64–65, 108–10, 128
missions, 89–91, 110–11
Mohawk, John, 21–22, 23
Moody Bible College, 12
Mother Earth, 73, 75
mound-building cultures, 28–29, 31

naming, 57
narrative/stories, 46–48, 61, 93
  fact and, 107–8
  scripture, 50–51, 102–3, 126
  theology, 20–21, 62–63
nationalism, 46–47
Native American cultural contextual
  movement, 126–27
Navajo, 91
New Zealand, 72, 95
Nez Perce, 133
Niehoff, Arthur, 65

Ohiyesa, Charles Eastman, 74
Ojibwa, 5–6, 10–13
  spiritual leaders, 12–13
oppression, 3, 83
  racial, 14, 36–37, 71, 73–74, 120
  of women, 3, 83
oral tradition, 11, 86, 93, 102, 125–26
  spoken words, 62–63, 93, 98

Pacific Northwest, 30
Painter, Nell Irvin, 23
panentheism, 65, 77
pedagogy, Indigenized, 20–21, 47–48,
  131
Pequot, 34, 64–65
physics, 49–50, 77
Pilgrims, 33–34, 97
plants, 55–56
Portland Seminary, 1–2
post-colonial stress disorder (PCSD),
  35, 81
  intergenerational trauma, 35, 36
post-traumatic stress disorder
  (PTSD), 35, 81, 133–34

poverty, 15–16, 83, 120
power, illegitimate use of, 10
powwows, 112–13, 114, 128
pre-colonial civilizations, 25–30
privilege, 13–17, 71, 83, 108, 115
  White, 71, 102, 123
progressive civilization, 21–22
propositional thinking, 102–3
Pueblo, 29

quarks, 49–50

racism, 14, 36–37, 71, 120
  solutions, 73–74
Rather, Dan, 42–43
reality, 58–59, 61–62, 63, 67, 78
  categorization and, 63–64, 99–100
  partial, 99–100
  virtual, 111–12
redemption, 79
relationships, 41–43
reparations, 42–43, 74, 81–82, 103
Revolutionary War, 17–18
Ricoeur, Paul, 84
rituals, 128–29, 131–32, 134
Rockefeller, John D., 102
Rome, 21, 23, 26, 98, 100–101, 120
  church structure, 100–101

salvation, 68–69, 73, 79, 87–88,
  99–101, 109–10
Schillebeeckx, Edward, 100n3
scripture, 35, 50–51
  Indigenous people and, 50–51,
  125–26
  interpretation of, 46–47, 57–58,
  84–86, 126–27

Jesus and, 23–24, 25, 48
    narrative, 50–51, 102–3, 126
Seattle, Chief, 53–54
Selu and Kanati, 59
Seneca, 21
settler people, 32, 42–43, 53–54,
    81–82, 128–29
shalom, 68–70, 71–72, 85–87, 95–97,
    98–103, 134
Shoshone, 132
Six Nations, 21, 22n13
Smith, Christian, 73–74
Smith, Linda, 72
Smith, Redbird, 69
Sonoran Desert, 26, 29–30
Spirit, 5, 77–78, 107, 111
spirituality, 51–52, 61–62, 73, 82–83,
    92, 123
    leaders, 12–13, 47–48, 81
spiritual teaching, 11–12, 103
Starkloff, Carl, 33
stomp dance culture, 5, 47–48
stories. See narrative/stories
Sun, Creator and, 47–48
sweat lodges, 52, 113, 122–23, 124,
    132–33
symbols, 92, 132–34
syncretism, 110–11
systems, 20–21, 58, 70, 95–96, 100
    change of, 104–6, 115–16
    racism, 35, 81

Tellico, 15–16
Tennessee, University of, 15–16
Teresa, Mother, 42–43
Terrapin and the wolves, 17–18, 24
theology/theologians, 7, 78, 80
    dualism, 72–73
    European, 62, 71

history and, 14–17
Indigenous, 20–21, 61–66, 77–78,
    80, 110–11, 121–22
Indigenous narrative, 62, 120
of land / of place, 58, 65–68, 120
liberation, 115–16
narrative, 20–21, 62–63
salvation, 68–69, 73, 79, 87–88,
    99–101
Trickster, 71, 80
Trinity, 62, 78, 86–87
    Community of Creator, 49–50,
    86–87
truth, 46–47, 61, 68, 71–72, 106
    conversion to, 108–9
    experience and, 62–63, 92
    Jesus Christ and, 72, 88
    story and, 107–8
Turtle, Grandmother, 38–41
Turtle Island, 10, 30, 40–41

Underhill, Captain John, 64–65
United Nations Declaration on the
    Rights of Indigenous Peoples
    (UNDRIP), 36
urbanization, 60, 75–76, 114–15
utopia, 58, 60–61, 100–101

values studies, 90–94, 130
vulnerability, 103–4, 105

Wampanoag, 33–34
Western worldview, 20–22, 41–43,
    61–65, 77–78, 97–99, 111, 120–21
White people, 122–23, 128–29
    Bible translation, 50, 125–26
    superiority, 36–37, 81
    supremacy, 21, 101–2, 103

Williams, Robert, 23
Wind River Indian Reservation, WY, 6
Winthrop, John, 64
women, 3, 75, 83, 93
words, 24, 63, 98, 106
  spoken, 62–63, 93, 98
  written, 46, 50–51, 63, 84, 101, 122,
    125–26
worldviews, 3–5
  conquest, 62–63, 64–65, 70–72
  European, 41–42, 71, 101, 122–23

experience and, 122–24
harmony based, 72–74
holistic, 62, 75–76, 98–99, 122
Indigenous, 61–65, 90–95, 98–99
of Jesus, 46, 73
Western, 20–22, 41–43, 61–65,
  77–78, 97–99, 111, 120–21

YWAM Native leadership, 10–11